Table of Contents

This book is to be returned on or before
the last date stamped below.

2 5 SEP 1998

WITHDRAWN

LIBREX

FRANCIS HOLLAND SCHOOL LIBRARY
CLARENCE GATE, LONDON NW1 6XR

First published in July 1996

by

THE ENVIRONMENT UNIT
THE INSTITUTE OF ECONOMIC AFFAIRS

2 Lord North Street, Westminster,
London SW1P 3LB

Studies on the Environment No. 7

ISBN 0-255 36383-4

Set in Plantin and Univers

Printed in Great Britain by
Goron Pro-Print Co Ltd, Lancing, W. Sussex

Foreword

The IEA's publication of *Down to Earth: A Contrarian View of Environmental Problems* by Dr Matt Ridley in February 1995 coincided serendipitously with that of *Small is Stupid: Blowing the Whistle on the Greens* by Wilfred Beckerman (Duckworth, 1995) and *Life on a Modern Planet: A Manifesto for Progress* by Richard North (Manchester University Press, 1995). The result of three 'contrarian' books appearing at the same time was quite spectacular. 'So, the end isn't nigh' proclaimed *The Daily Telegraph*; 'Apocalypse Never' wrote *The Guardian*; and 'Spate of sceptical books provokes Green backlash' reported *The Independent*.

Whether the publication of *Down to Earth II* achieves such headline recognition is yet to be seen but it is certainly deserved. Too many sequels are but pale imitations of their forerunners. However in this case, a superb collection that I was proud to see the IEA publish is followed by a second anthology which even surpasses the first.

This collection is a real treat. The reader's sense of comedy will be engaged far more than is usual in an IEA text. But the sense of the ridiculous will soon give way to a sense of danger: behind the fashionable environmental fads Ridley challenges lies a common thread of powerful vested interests, interests which seek to direct our lives.

But (as well as having a Ph.D. in Zoology) Ridley knows his economics - in particular Public Choice Theory, that body of thought which invites us to enquire into the hidden beneficiaries of different policy alternatives. Scientific reports inevitably recommend policy prescriptions that deliver bigger budgets, higher salaries, pensions and perks to those calling for more government.

As the big idea called 'central planning' is discredited, some of its close cousins in the world of ideas become more active every day. 'Save the Whales' is a compelling slogan: everyone wants to do so. The whaling industry above all others needs a

5

healthy stock. However, glib slogans omit just how we can best protect such marine mammals and their land-based counterparts.

The African elephants and rhinos* would surely be better served if they were owned by people with a pecuniary interest in their survival and welfare rather than being owned by nobody and prey to poaching. Likewise the best way to conserve fish is to create property rights over them. Either access to fishing waters can be sold or the fish themselves can be confined to a limited area. Without clear property rights in land and livestock we would have no modern agricultural industry – without property rights in the seabed and the fish, fishing is still conducted on a Stone Age basis.

The main lesson of Dr Ridley's analysis is that by and large we are in good shape; that where problems exist it is because of a lack of ownership rights, markets and the rule of law; that applying such principles provides clear, workable solutions to environmental problems; and that we have good reasons to distrust the motives of the grant-seeking greens, vote-maximising politicians and budget-enhancing bureaucrats and scientists. Matt Ridley originally wrote these essays for the ephemeral world of journalism. It is impressive that they endure beyond their month of publication. Partly this is because the errors he combats are recurring ones. Partly it is the sheer intelligence of the author that keeps us propelled by the logic and the charm of his phrasing.

This volume includes 34 of Dr Ridley's *Sunday Telegraph* columns 'Down to Earth', and 6 additional articles taken from *The Sunday Telegraph*, *The Daily Telegraph*, *Literary Review*, *The Times* and *The World in 1996* (© The Economist Publications). The selections from 'Down to Earth' appear as originally written and so in some cases may differ from the printed version. The other articles appear as printed.

The 'Down to Earth' columns are reproduced in association with and by permission of *The Sunday Telegraph*. Additional articles are published with the permission of *The Daily*

---

* See *Elephants and Ivory: Lessons from the Trade Ban* by Ike Sugg and Urs Kreuter (IEA Studies on the Environment No. 2, November 1994) and *Rhinos: Conservation, Economics and Trade-Offs* by Michael 't Sas-Rolfes (IEA Studies on the Environment No. 4, April 1995).

Telegraph, Literary Review, The Times and © The Economist Publications. The IEA acknowledges their co-operation.

The views expressed in this IEA publication are those of the author, not of the Institute (which has no corporate view), its Trustees, Directors or Advisers. It is published as a contribution to the debate on how best to protect the environment.

June 1996   JOHN BLUNDELL
                     General Director, Institute of Economic Affairs

The Author

Matt Ridley's last book *The Red Queen* was short listed for the Rhone-Poulenc prize for science books and the Writers Guild Award for non-fiction. He obtained his DPhil in zoology from Oxford University; worked as science editor, Washington correspondent and American editor for *The Economist*; and created the successful 'Down to Earth' column for the London *Sunday Telegraph*. A research fellow of the Institute of Economic Affairs and a Trustee of the International Centre for Life, Dr Ridley lives in Northumberland with his wife, who is a university lecturer, and his son.

Acknowledgements

I would like to thank Lisa Mac Lellan, Roger Bate and John Blundell at the Institute of Economic Affairs for all their support and encouragement. Thanks also to the editors who originally published these articles, especially Charles Moore and Jon Connell.

M.R.

PART I

ECONOMIC SOLUTIONS

1. Perverse Incentives and Fisheries*

Jorge Luis Borges once compared the Falklands war to two bald men fighting over a comb. The argument between the British and the Spanish fishing fleets over the Irish box has something of the same quality. It is blatantly evident that far too many fish are already being caught in Europe's waters and that the squabble is about who shall profit from commercially exterminating the stock. Yet there is no excuse for Europe to mismanage its fisheries so; the biology and economics of fishery management are simple (the politics are another matter).

Our fishermen regard their fishing opportunities as a right that they have acquired by investing in trawlers. British fishermen are therefore furious at having to donate some of their rights to Spaniards and are demanding that they be compensated by us taxpayers for leaving the industry instead.

If the government were to limit British car production to allow Spanish imports more chance, the car industry would rightly be aggrieved. Fish are different, because only a limited number can be caught without destroying the stock. Therefore the chance to catch fish is not an infinitely expandable right, but a privilege, a share in a monopoly franchise, and as such it should be sold on behalf of us taxpayers to the highest bidder.

The British government is actually doing this quite successfully around the Falkland Islands, where it charges as much as the market will bear for the chance to catch squid and fish, thus earning more for the islands than all their sheep put together. It is able to do this because the fishing fleet is foreign, and politics does not enter the question.

The politically easier alternative is to reduce the fishing season in length until it is too short for over-exploitation. Off Alaska, this approach has led to seasons so short they are measured in days (halibut) or even minutes (herring roe). But

---

* Published as 'Fish 'n' ships Euro recipe is hard to digest' in *The Sunday Telegraph* on 15 January 1995.

11

time-limited fishing has two drawbacks. It encourages fishermen to chase other species in other seasons, which brings pressure to bear elsewhere, and it places no incentives on fishermen to do anything other than catch as much as they can, if necessary by cheating the rules, which in turn imposes huge policing costs on the taxpayer for no reward.

New South Wales has just begun to implement a system that should avoid these difficulties. It allocates shares in a fishery to each fisherman based on his past catch, for free. But these shares become fully transferable permanent titles to a proportion of the fishery. Each year the government sets the absolute size of the catch. To pay for the system and allow new entrants to the business, each fishermen must surrender 2·5 per cent of his quota back to the government each year – although he can then buy it back.

Fishermen now own an asset – the quota – against which they can borrow to invest. In a year when the total catch was set low, the price of quota would fall; in a year when it was high it would rise. The effect is to give the fishermen a stake in keeping stocks high, to treat them as part owners of the resource, rather than competitors in a scramble to mine it. If they are caught cheating they lose a large part of their quota.

Mike Young, who devised the system for the New South Wales government, tells me that Iceland is hoping to copy it. There is nothing to stop Europe doing so as well. Nothing that is, except its philosophy, which is that individuals are not to be trusted with property, only institutions and states. Hence the Common Fisheries Policy, which so enrages our fishermen by confiscating their hard-earned share and granting it to Spanish rivals, a measure that could not be better designed to encourage the near extermination of the cod in the Irish box.

2. The Disastrous Common Agricultural Policy*

The achievements of the Common Agricultural Policy of the European Union are truly remarkable. Although the cost to the taxpayer and consumer has risen steadily for 20 years, reaching several billion pounds last year just in Britain, look what you have got for your money! Less contribution to the economy: agricultural output has fallen by half as a proportion of Europe's GDP since 1973. Fewer farmers: employment in agriculture has also halved. More dependence on taxpayers: subsidies now account for 66 per cent of the gross value added in agriculture, compared with 9 per cent in 1973. More regulation: public bureaucrats now effectively control many decisions made on farms. More environmental damage: lapwing populations are down by 47 per cent since 1969 and there are 30 per cent fewer plant species on farmland. And regressive redistribution: since farmers are on average richer than consumers, the policy robs the poor to pay the rich.

As disastrous returns on investment go, this counts up there with the South Sea Bubble. Little wonder that reform of the CAP is suddenly all the rage – even in France. True, it was reformed in 1992 but that only made future reform more likely by transferring the cost of support from the consumer (who can be trusted not to notice that bread costs more in Europe than America) to the taxpayer. So the incoming European agriculture commissioner, Herr Franz Fischler of Austria, has fair wind.

There is hardly a pressure group in the country, from the National Farmers' Union to the Council for the Protection of Rural England and the Country Landowners' Association, that is not actively promoting some suggestion for CAP reform. What is more remarkable is that they are all unanimous on the direction that reform should take. They urge the politicians to

---

* Published as 'Time to uproot the cash crop that never fails' in *The Sunday Telegraph* on 22 January 1995.

13

switch subsidies from paying for farm produce to paying for environmental benefits.

It would all be very cosy. The farmers go on collecting £200 every time they pass go, while the greens consult and advise and collect fees, and the bureaucrats still justify their existence by handing out huge sums and then tut-tutting over the need to enforce labour-intensive measures against fraud (requiring bigger budgets). The taxpayer, good little obedient chap that he is, would be told that he benefited because he would have more lapwings to look at – and he would prefer that, surely, to tax cuts.

Sorry to spoil the party, fellows, but to abolish the CAP rather than reform it would provide the same benefits at lower cost. The abolition of subsidies would cut taxes, cut food prices, stop distorting world trade and make European farm exports more competitive. Yes, you say, but at a terrible price. Many farmers would go bust; and the ones that did not would pour on the fertiliser and chemicals to boost yields, doing the lapwings even more harm.

This is conventional wisdom and, as usual, conventional wisdom is wrong. There is no industry in the world that responds to falling prices for its products by spending more on making them. As the example of the United States amply demonstrates, when wheat prices are lower, farmers use less chemicals, not more, and accept lower yields. Result: more lapwings, not fewer. And if Europe stopped dumping exports on to the world market, world prices for cereals would rise, to a point at which price most European growers could compete.

The example of New Zealand, which suddenly removed all farm subsidies in one swoop, is encouraging. Many fewer farmers went under or left the industry than expected, and farming became noticeably less intensive and therefore more wildlife-friendly.

Of course, the bureaucrats, lobbyists and other jackals that scavenge for taxpayers' money wherever government spills it might have to 'downsize' their operations. What a pity.

3. How to Wipe Out a Pest – Put a Price on its Head*

Alien pests have probably driven more species extinct than all mankind's other effects put together. Rats, cats, pigs, rabbits, foxes and others have wiped out the unique native fauna of islands across the world and devastated that of Australia and New Zealand. Most such pests originate in Europe, but there are some North American ones that have been just as harmful here. The grey squirrel, which is steadily wiping out the native red, is one example.

The mink is another. Mink thrive along many British river banks where they are now known to have locally extirpated water voles (of Wind in the Willows fame), moorhens, dippers and many other much loved species. I suggest a scheme for the extermination of mink.

Ask any environmentalist and they will tell you it is impossible and we should learn to love the mink; what they mean is that they are terrified of ever suggesting that people should kill animals even if those animals are reducing biodiversity as mink are doing. But animal sentimentalism is not conservation. There is no reason why a simple bounty scheme, rewarding people for killing mink, should not work.

But bounty schemes have been tried in the past and failed, you say. In 1952, a one-shilling bounty on grey squirrels produced 168,000 claims, but grey squirrels increased nonetheless. Yes, but the schemes have always had a crucial flaw: the law of diminishing returns. They get less and less effective as a species gets rarer and more wary.

My scheme is a fixed-pool bounty divided between all claimants. It would work as follows. Somebody (perhaps the government, perhaps not) would put up a fixed sum every year, of say £1 million. This would then be divided by the number of mink pelts sent in. Suppose in the first year, because of poor

***

* Published in *The Sunday Telegraph* on 29 January 1995.

15

publicity, only 20,000 pelts are sent in. Each pelt would then be worth £50. This windfall would soon alert gamekeepers and others to the rewards of killing mink.

If the pool was too small, it might merely cause a perpetual harvest of mink that never damaged the stock. But the beauty of the scheme is that there would always be a pool size that would cause the price to start to rise and it would never stop rising. For, as the mink grew scarcer, the price per pelt would rise ever higher, so the effort expended to catch another animal would rise accordingly. The price would then rise steadily year by year until by the end the last mink in Britain would have a bounty of a million pounds on its head.

The principle is exactly the same as that behind the extinction of the beaver in much of North America between 1700 and 1900: the scarcer beavers grew, the more valuable they became. Once the price per mink pelt had risen to, say, £1,000, some people would devote much of their spare time to mink trapping. Indeed, one of the benefits of such a scheme is that it would give unemployed people a chance of earning a bonus windfall, rather than the money going to those already in employment. Most landowners would readily grant freelance mink trappers access to their land.

There would, of course, be problems, and bureaucrats will no doubt devote much energy to thinking of them. Fraud, for example, would be a problem, as people raided mink farms for pelts. But why not decree that all captive mink have their tails docked or numbers tattooed on their ears at birth? This would have the added advantage of allowing the identification and prosecution of those farms that allow mink to escape. Administration expenses need not be great: one secretary to count pelts and enter addresses on the computer, one day of reckoning at the end of the year. Does English Nature have the courage to adopt such a scheme?

4. Hydrogen, the Fuel of the Future[*]

Every forecaster since Malthus has underestimated the effect of new technology. Horses to cars, whale oil to petroleum, copper cables to optical fibres, steelmaking to software – the transitions from one technology to another have relentlessly caught out the unwary environmental pessimists in every generation. The techno-optimists have been wrong, too, but in detail rather than in principle.

Recklessly, therefore, I am about to predict the future of world energy supplies. By the middle of the next century, I think, the world will run largely on hydrogen. My confidence is based on an extraordinary chart drawn up by an Italian engineer, Cesare Marchetti, ten years ago.

Human fuel consists almost exclusively of two elements, hydrogen and carbon. If it is food we call it carbohydrate and burn it in our cells; if it is fossil fuel we call it hydrocarbon and burn it in our engines. Marchetti's graph shows the ratio of carbon to hydrogen in the average human fuel since 1850. Plotted on a log scale, it shows a dead straight line from four-to-one carbon to hydrogen in 1850 to two-to-one hydrogen to carbon today. Extrapolate the graph and we will be burning almost pure hydrogen by the year 2050.

The reason we are gradually shifting from carbon to hydrogen is that we are gradually changing the fuel we use. Until about 1890, the most common fuel in the world was wood, which is one part hydrogen and 99 parts carbon. Between 1890 and 1960 coal was the dominant fuel; coal is about one-to-one carbon to hydrogen. Since 1960 oil has been the dominant fuel; it is about two-to-one hydrogen to carbon. But natural gas is rapidly displacing oil, and it is four parts hydrogen to one part carbon. Every switch is towards hydrogen.

---

[*] Published as 'Hydrogen really will go down a bomb' in *The Sunday Telegraph* on 26 March 1995.

The next step is obvious: to hydrogen itself. It is easy enough to make by electrolysing water using solar power or other sources of electricity. Only cost prevents us from churning it out in vast quantities: liquid hydrogen currently costs four times as much as petrol. But the cost of solar power is falling steadily and shows no sign of hitting the bottom yet.

If – and I will be a very old man when proved wrong in 2050 – hydrogen replaces natural gas as the main fuel in the middle of the next century, it will of course solve the problem of global warming. Burnt hydrogen (which we call water) is an even more powerful greenhouse gas than burnt carbon (which we call carbon dioxide). But the atmosphere automatically rids itself of excess water vapour by shedding it in a familiar form, which we call rain. So, in a world of pure hydrogen-burning there would be no build-up of greenhouse gases.

This is one reason why the latest government wheeze for wasting taxpayers' money is so absurd. It consists of subsidies for landowners to grow coppiced willow and harvest it regularly for new wood-burning power stations. The programme is being touted as green, because the fuel is renewable and the carbon dioxide it generates has been fixed from the atmosphere, not taken out of the ground.

In practice, though, carbon dioxide is carbon dioxide, whether it came from plants that grew yesterday or 200 million years ago (coal). Planting trees to mop carbon dioxide out of the atmosphere makes some sense as a green measure if you then bury them underground or launch them into outer space; burning them again has no virtue. Besides, since wood is 99 per cent carbon and 1 per cent hydrogen, it is the most disastrous fuel to encourage if you are worried about carbon dioxide. The money would be better spent enabling people who currently burn wood, in the third world mainly, to switch to a hydrogen-rich fuel such as natural gas.

5. Australia Banks on Trick Sperm to Kill Off Rabbits*

The spread of genetically engineered viruses that cause sterilisation sounds more like the plot of Michael Crichton's next novel than a serious proposal. But it is in fact one of the most promising, if risky, new ideas in conservation, albeit ten years from actual use.

The idea is quite simple: to infect a rabbit with a virus that makes it immune to its own sperm and watch that rabbit infect other rabbits. An epidemic of sterility would then pass through rabbits, humanely and painlessly reducing their numbers to the great benefit of their economic and ecological victims: farmers, trees, and in Australia, rare native species of plant and animal. Rabbits would then be spared the attention of shotguns and cyanide, so they too would be happier. Only the unconceived would 'suffer'.

In the laboratory, the principle seems to work. It is quite easy to fool the body's immune system into thinking that sperm is an invading germ, and attacking it. Indeed, some people are rendered sterile by a natural mistake of this sort on the part of their body.

Likewise, it is proving possible to get vaccines to hitch-hike on viruses. Throughout Europe, for example, rabies is now kept under close control by dropping from helicopters fox bait tainted with a virus containing rabies vaccine. In this case the virus dies soon after the fox catches it, so there is no infection from fox to fox, but the fox is rendered immune to rabies.

So all that is needed is to put the two together and stick a 'genetic contraceptive' in a virus. This is what the Australians are starting to do at their Vertebrate Biocontrol Centre near Canberra, using the myxoma virus, which causes myxomatosis.

---

* Published as 'Aussies bank on trick sperm to kill off rabbits' in *The Sunday Telegraph* on 9 April 1995.

Only rabbits can catch myxomatosis; not even hares get it. So there is no chance of the sterility spreading from rabbits to other creatures. Also, the chemical recognition between sperm and egg is so precisely different in each species that even if the virus were to spread to other species its sterilising effect almost certainly would not.

The risk of an unintended effect, even a mass sterilisation of human beings, is therefore vanishingly small. To be safe, though, governments are likely to insist that none of these experiments will be allowed in the wild until every possible risk has been tested in captivity. Even such controlled tests are still many years away. A far greater risk is that the technique simply will not work. After all, the virus will have to compete with 'wild' viruses that are probably better adapted to spreading from rabbit to rabbit.

Moreover, the myxomatosis epidemics of the 1950s and 1960s eventually lost their virulence as rabbits developed immunity. The same natural selection would go to work with an immuno-virus, as those rabbits that did not catch it left more offspring than those that did. So the virus would have to be frequently reinvented to continue working – another reason it is not as dangerous an idea as it first sounds.

Even so, the Australians, fighting to save their native wildlife from competition with introduced rabbits, foxes, cats and rats, regard 'viral-vectored' contraception as having the potential to 'change the face of Australian conservation.' In Britain, too, it might also prove a valuable conservation tool, to moderate the fecundity of introduced pests that are threatening our native wildlife, such as grey squirrels and mink. One day.

6. Markets, not Governments, Solve Overfishing*

'The cod fishery, the herring fishery, the pilchard fishery, the mackerel fishery, and probably all the great sea fisheries are inexhaustible.' Thus wrote Thomas Henry Huxley in 1883, reminding us that he was one of those people who was wrong almost as often as he was right.

Fisheries are the most blatantly exhaustible resource on the planet. Conservationists and Canadians are right and Spaniards and Brusselcrats are wrong: fish need far more intrusive protection.

However, it was a bit rich to be lectured on this topic in last Saturday's *Daily Telegraph* by Jonathan Porritt, who had taken exception to some things I and two other authors had said on the subject of greens. Having admitted that we contrarians were often right that greens were often wrong in their apocalyptic predictions, Porritt then demanded credit for where they have been right. He gave an example: fish.

Good, Jonathan, let us talk about fish, since they are in the news. The average catch in the early 1970s was about 65 million tonnes; it is now about 95 million tonnes, down from its all time peak of 100 million tonnes in 1989. It is therefore a very poor example to choose to illustrate devastation and apocalypse. But perhaps we have only just begun to overdo it. (So far, so good, said the man falling past the tenth floor of the Empire State Building.)

So let us give the alarmists the benefit of the doubt and accept that world fish catches are about to collapse suddenly from their unsustainable levels, as so many local fisheries have often done. Jonathan Porritt asserts that only greens have been predicting this, in the teeth of complacency from economists.

---

* Published as 'The Greens are not using their loaves on fish' in *The Sunday Telegraph* on 16 April 1995.

Not so. It was a Canadian economist, Scott Gordon, in 1954 when Greenpeace was not even a glint in its father's eye, who first pointed out the problem with fisheries, and why they tended inevitably to collapse from overfishing. And it was economists in the early 1990s who first showed that they could prevent that collapse.

The entire problem with fisheries is one of ownership. Because nobody on the high seas can easily stop anybody else catching fish, a free-for-all develops. Restraint by one fisherman merely leaves more for others to catch. 'Wealth that is free for all is valued by none,' wrote Gordon.

Yet regulation of net sizes, fishing limits or boat numbers, the solution urged on us endlessly by greens, has almost everywhere been a stunning failure, most spectacularly in the case of the European Common Fisheries Policy. Why? Because politicians have every incentive to be lenient and fishermen to cheat.

Market-based solutions, urged by economists, have on the other hand been immediate successes. Everybody who studies fishing seriously now agrees that the only way to run a fishery sustainably is to stop thinking that the government or the European Union must own the fish and let the fishermen own it. Grant or auction shares in a flexibly regulated total catch to the fishermen, let them sell those shares on to others if they wish and thereby give each fisherman an incentive to police the system so as to preserve and enhance the value of his share. The better each fisherman behaves, the greater the value of his investment. It is, if you like, a form of privatisation, and it is sweeping the world. New South Wales has the best system, which Iceland is now copying. New Zealand has almost as good a system, and the Falklands version is working especially well.

Fishing therefore proves exactly the point that we contrarians have been making in the teeth of different advice from greens: use the market, not the bureaucracy, to solve environmental problems. If it is the best example the greens can find to refute our case, then our case must be even stronger than I thought it was.

7. Denmark, the Great Hypocrite of Greenery*

If hypocrisy was selling for £50 a barrel, the North Sea would have been a valuable place last week. Top of the list of hypocrites comes Greenpeace, which decided to play silly games in wet suits and helicopters not to save the environment, but to reverse an alarming fall in their membership from nearly 5 million people in 1990 to less than 3 million this year.

Hypocrisy poured out of Germany and Holland, which produce more lead in ten minutes from the mouth of the Rhine than is in the Brent Spar installation. But the biggest deposits of hypocrisy are in the Danish sector of the North Sea. The Danish prime minister, Poul Nyrop Rasmussen, sent an official protest to John Major, said he would not buy Shell petrol and said the plan to sink the Brent Spar was 'against the environmental consciousness of Danish families'.

Let us examine Mr Rasmussen's precious environmental consciousness in a little more detail. The North Sea's biggest environmental problem by far is not oil, but overfishing (to which, to forestall charges of hypocrisy, I must to confess to having contributed last week, when I caught three delicious cod). Overfishing is caused by greedy fishermen of all nations, who bend the rules, catch more than they should, sell the excess fish for cash to the East European Klondyker fleets and so forth. But there is one egregious cause of overfishing: Denmark's industrial fishing fleet, which destructively and indiscriminately hoovers up fish that are not even destined for eating by people.

The fish are fed to pigs and cows (yes, cows!) and crushed to make oil that is fed to power stations to make electricity. Correction: fish oil is not being burnt in power stations at the moment because the price is too high, but the contracts for it are still out and it soon will be again if the price drops.

---

* Published in *The Sunday Telegraph* on 25 June 1995.

These splendidly futile reasons for catching fish that could otherwise be feeding people, seals or birds are only the beginning of Denmark's and Mr Rasmussen's tale of hypocrisy. The Danes grow fish-fattened cows and pigs in such numbers for their vast food-exporting industry that their manure causes serious 'run-off' pollution of nutrients from the fields. This pours into the sea, where 'eutrophication' results, algal blooms spread across the shallow sea, breeding ground of so many fish, and starve marine life of oxygen.

However, you will find no trace of this run-off problem in Denmark's pollution statistics. Why not? Because the Danes do not measure it. There are two ways of measuring how much you pollute the sea. The British way is to measure the water itself – levels of pollutants as they enter the sea. The Danish way is to measure only emissions – the outfalls of sewage farms and add them up. Since agricultural run-off does not go through sewage farms, hey presto the Danish figure for pollution appears lower than the British.

Mr Rasmussen has not finished yet. He gets special exemptions for importing whale meat from Greenland. Under the climate change convention, he has fiddled the figures on carbon dioxide to be allowed to increase his country's already high per-capita carbon dioxide production by the amount of electricity his country imported from Norway, thus taking part of the Norwegian allowance. This is not a green politician, let alone one with an 'environmental consciousness'.

Fair enough if he thinks whaling is right, carbon dioxide is good, marine pollution should be encouraged and overfishing does not matter. But for such a man to lecture the rest of us about the infinitesimal problem of pollution that could have resulted from sinking the Brent Spar – a decision which he rubber-stamped – is rich indeed.

PART II

MYTHS, DUBIOUS SCIENCE AND THE ENVIRONMENT

8. White Lies and Melting Ice Caps*

'That iceberg,' said a taxi driver to me the other day, 'The one that's broken off a whole ice shelf in the Antarctic, now that's serious.' He proceeded to terrify me with a detailed account of all the dire things that will happen when the level of the sea rises after the ice caps melt.

Since there seems to be unanimous agreement that the climate of the Antarctic Peninsula has indeed got quite rapidly warmer since the 1950s, and since the ice shelfs around the peninsula are now clearly shrinking, there is little doubt that we are seeing global warming in action. No great surprise in that: the globe has been getting warmer for more than a century, largely because of natural effects, and despite some contradictory signals, the balance of probability is that it still is getting slowly warmer.

But beware the doomsayers of rising sea levels. Before you feel too worried for Venice and Bangladesh, it is worth bearing several pertinent facts in mind. The first is that ice shelves are mostly afloat. If they break up and melt, they do not raise sea level at all, because, like Archimedes's body in the bath, they take up just as much space as the same weight of water would. The fragmentation of Antarctica's ice shelves may have all sorts of other effects, but it will not itself cause sea levels to rise. The same goes for the Arctic sea ice.

What is more, there is something almost amounting to a consensus that in a warmer world, more moisture in the warmer air would cause more snow on Antarctica and therefore more of the sea's water would be exported on to the ice cap, reducing sea level. That is what happened seven thousand years ago, when global temperatures suddenly rose by about two degrees. Obviously, this might be offset by a sudden collapse into the sea of a whole continental ice cap, but it seems unlikely on present knowledge. So the only safe course of action is to take a large

---

* Published as 'Cool down – the oceans shall not inherit the Earth' in *The Sunday Telegraph* on 5 March 1995.

27

pinch of salt with any confident prediction anybody makes about the effect of small changes in climate on ice caps.

Talking of experts, it is worth comparing what they were solemnly telling us just a few short years ago with what they now say about sea level. In 1980 they said sea level would rise by eight metres over the next century because of global warming. In 1989, they said one metre. In 1990, in the guise of the Intergovernmental Panel on Climate Change, they were down to 65 centimetres (assuming a rise in global temperatures of four degrees). In 1993 an authoritative estimate was that sea level would rise 20 centimetres in a century if carbon dioxide levels quadrupled because of thermal expansion of existing seawater, but that the effects of melting ice were simply impossible to estimate. In other words, don't know.

Even so, a few feet of extra sea could make all the difference to some people's safety. It sounds scary for a country like the Maldives, which is mostly less than two metres above sea level, or Bangladesh, 20 per cent of which is within two metres of sea level. But remember these are estimates of how much it might rise gradually during the next century. Raising sea walls by a few feet over a whole century is not, surely, an impossible challenge.

Besides, our distant ancestors lived through the ice age, during which sea level fell by about three hundred feet, and then rose quite quickly by about the same amount to its present level. Never let it be said that we cannot cope with a problem 1 per cent as large as one that did not faze Neanderthal man.

9. How Seat-belts Add Danger to your Driving[*]

Had Brian Mawhinney announced three weeks ago that school minibuses would have to use seat-belts, I would have applauded him. Like almost everybody else, I thought compulsory wearing of seat-belts saved lives and were therefore worth having, even at the expense of a little lost liberty.

But then I was asked to review a new book, *Risk* by John Adams of University College in London, and I have utterly changed my mind. If past experience is anything to go by, Dr Mawhinney has just unwittingly increased the chances of fatal accidents involving school minibuses.

You think I have gone mad? On average, seat-belts do save lives if you are in a crash; there is no doubt about that. But the statistics unambiguously show that they also make accidents more likely, not less, and that this more than compensates for the other effect.

Do you feel slightly less safe if for some reason you are driving without a seat-belt? Do you therefore take a sharp bend slightly more slowly? More to the point, do you think other people react this way?

In 1981, just before Britain made seat-belts compulsory, the government thought the measure would save one life for every 250 million kilometres travelled. Therefore the reassurance that seat-belts give to other drivers has only to increase your chances of an accident by one crash every 250 million kilometres, and you are worse off.

Between 1988 and 1990 the number of people killed and injured on the roads rose by about six per cent (it's not clear why). The number of children killed and injured in the rear seats of cars rose over the same period by 10 and 12 per cent respectively – twice as fast. In 1989 rear seat-belts were made compulsory for children.

---

[*] Published in *The Sunday Telegraph* on 19 March 1995.

Fluke statistic, you say. Well, why is it that the countries that made front seat-belts compulsory in the 1970s saw a slower decrease in accident rates than the countries that did not? Why is it that Australia, the first country to make seat-belts compulsory, was the only country in a large sample that saw an increase in road deaths in the late 1970s? Why is it that the 27 American states which relaxed their laws forcing motorcyclists to wear helmets in the late 1970s saw a significantly smaller increase in motorcycle fatalities than the 23 states which did not relax their laws?

This effect is known as risk compensation. In one study, Swedish drivers using studded tyres in icy conditions rounded a bend faster than those who used normal tyres. The Davy Lamp killed more miners than it saved because its 'safety' encouraged risk taking in the mines. Children were more likely to be killed playing in the road in the 1920s than today, because roads were 'safer': today people do not let their children play in the road. In Germany, the drivers of buses with seat-belts are actually allowed by law to travel faster than those without.

If these statistical assertions by John Adams are true, how come the consensus of safety experts is so firmly in favour of seat-belts? The answer, as so often, is that conventional wisdom is simply wrong, and is supported not by the facts but by its own partisan momentum. Adams's results were confirmed by a Department of Transport study, which was then suppressed. He and others who agree with him are simply shouted down whenever they point out such facts.

Yet facts are facts. Seat-belts make accidents more survivable; they do not reduce the risk of them happening. The logical thing to do to reduce the risk of accidents for school minibuses is to make it compulsory for the drivers *not* to wear a seat-belt. That will ensure that they take more care.

10. Beware of the Greens Who Cry Wolf*

The past month has seen the coincidental publication of three books critical of environmentalists. Richard North's *Life on a Modern Planet*, Wilfred Beckerman's *Small is Stupid* and my own *Down to Earth* have been seen in some quarters almost as a concerted backlash. We have become the anti-greens.

This is horribly misleading. I think of myself as an environmentalist, and from North's and Beckerman's books, it is clear that they do too. That is why we share a revulsion at the hijacking of environmental issues by extremists who seem prepared to tell alarming fibs to get attention and market share in the competitive world of green charity. We also believe that regulation, state interference and centralisation are often the problem, not the solution; and that growth and technology are often the solution, not the problem.

Consider just a few of the dire predictions of environmentalists that have not come true. In 1968, Paul Ehrlich, a still respected eco-guru at Stanford University, wrote: "The fight to feed humanity is over. In the 1970s, the world will undergo famines – hundreds of millions of people are going to starve to death." Sixty-five million Americans would die of famine in the 1980s, he predicted. Per capita food production has risen; famine deaths have fallen steadily and those that do occur are caused by wars, not population pressure. Did Mr Ehrlich apologise?

In 1974, virtually everybody except the journalist Norman Macrae said the world would effectively run out of oil before the end of the century. Proven *reserves* of oil are now larger than ever before. It will run out one day, but fleets of alternative fuels are queuing up to take its place. Did anybody say they were wrong?

In 1976, three books predicted an imminent ice age and demanded immediate action to stave it off. The author of one,

---

* Published in *The Times* on 25 March 1995.

Stephen Schneider, has become a leading apocalyptic on global warming instead. He said in an unguarded moment: "Scientists should consider stretching the truth to get some broad-based support, to capture the public's imagination ... we have to offer up scary scenarios, make simplified dramatic statements, and make little mention of any doubts we might have." He did not say: "I was wrong ..."

In 1983, virtually everybody agreed that one-third of the trees in German forests were "dying" from acid rain. Not only did far fewer die, but a ten-year American study concluded that acid rain was not even at the top of the list of problems facing forests. Did the greens admit their error?

These are just the global scares we have been subjected to. On local ones, the greens have an even worse track record. The seals of the North Sea were supposed to be dying from pollution in 1989; they were actually suffering from a viral epidemic aided by high population density. The Braer oil spill last year was supposed to do irreparable damage to the wildlife of Shetland. Richard North and I were the only journalists to predict (correctly) that the effect would be minimal.

Greens say that it takes extreme statements to wake the public. Yet on none of the issues I have mentioned did green organisations begin the debate. They merely leapt on to bandwagons once they were moving. The truth is that the hyperbole is needed in a market competition for funds. Whether the issue is ozone, climate or ivory, moderate organisations have repeatedly seen their more mendacious rivals collect large windfalls of attention and donations, and have turned radical in response.

Scientists are also herd animals. On global warming, the attempt to silence doubters has reached such a point that no less a figure than the Vice-President of the United States, Al Gore, tried personally to discredit a global-warming sceptic, Fred Singer, by calling a television network and suggesting that Mr Singer was in the pay of industry and should not be interviewed. The network, to its credit, merely reported Mr Gore's intervention and interviewed Mr Singer anyway.

Do the means matter if the end is virtuous? Alarmists appeal to the "precautionary principle" – better safe than sorry. Yet, as

Beckerman argues, if we always acted to avoid the slightest risk, however uncertain, we would never get out of bed.

It is the imperviousness of the greens to such arguments that leads some to suspect them of the hidden motive to reinvent socialism. I think that, like all conspiracy theories, this is overdone, but it is nonetheless noticeable how reluctant most greens are even to consider environmental solutions that change the incentives for private individuals rather than impose government regulations. Empire-building bureaucrats love greens for this reason: they can rely on them to send work their way.

The nationalisation of wildlife in Africa, for instance, is dressed up as a protective measure. It is demonstrably the reverse, because while it gives jobs to the bureaucracy it removes incentives for local people to tolerate wildlife. Kenya banned hunting (ie, nationalised game) in 1976; since then it has lost 85 per cent of its elephants. Zimbabwe privatised wildlife in 1975; since then land devoted to wildlife has almost doubled in acreage.

It is the same in this country. It is the Government that has made a mess of things by subsidising farmers, foresters and old, heavy industry, and by regulations that stifle innovation. Even by criminalising pollution in 1960s, the Government effectively made it free (so long as each polluter did not exceed a certain threshold). Had it instead enabled the civil law to work cheaply so that we could sue polluters, or had it created a market in expensive pollution quotas, water and air pollution would be far less today than they are.

I am an environmentalist. There are issues I wish we would take more seriously, such as asthma, plastic litter, the decline of frogs and the loss of untouched rainforest to government-encouraged development. But I wish greens and lawmakers would try to devise real solutions that work with the grain of human nature, rather than whizzing round the world to glamorous conferences crying wolf about impending apocalypse.

11. Frogs and Ultra-violet Light*

Two weeks ago the pond in my garden was full of frogs laying their spawn. Two days of thick morning ice on the pond last week seems to have cooled their ardour, but they will probably be back. It is curious how much less tame they are than the toads, which will be there in April; the slightest glimpse of my approach and they dive. Frogs know they're good to eat; toads have the self-confidence of the poisonous.

There seems to be no shortage of both in the surrounding woods. But it is an undoubted fact that frogs and toads are growing scarcer throughout the world rather more rapidly than most other animals. The beautiful golden toad of Costa Rica simply vanished a few years ago, as did the gastric-brooding frog of Australia (which reared its tadpoles in its stomach). Many others are declining in number.

Why should frogs be so vulnerable? The answers are many and variable, of course. As in almost all conservation problems, the introduction of exotic competitors seems to be a big part of the problem: bullfrogs in parts of America and cane toads in Australia have driven out many native species. Fish are also big culprits. Frogs tend to live in places where fish cannot get to, but with man's help fish are being taken to places they cannot reach naturally, where the first thing they do is eat the tadpoles.

But the newest and most disturbing answer blames the damage to the ozone layer. In North-west America many of the frogs that have declined most steeply are those that breed in shallow water at higher altitudes, where ultra-violet light is most intense. After ruling out acid rain and water pollution, two scientists at Oregon State University began to suspect that ultra-violet light was the problem.

They set up an experiment in which frogspawn was put in three different kinds of mesh boxes, each floating free in a pond

---

* Published as 'Frogs' croak falls prey to ozone layer' in *The Sunday Telegraph* on 2 April 1995.

or lake. The first kind of box had an open top; the second had a plastic top transparent to all light; the third had a transparent top that blocked ultra-violet light only. The results were, in their word, 'dramatic'. About 40 per cent of the eggs of western toads and Cascade frogs failed to hatch in the boxes exposed to ultra-violet light, compared with 10-20 per cent of the eggs in the protected boxes.

Even more suggestive, Pacific tree frogs suffered no such effect: almost all their eggs hatched, whether covered or not. Pacific tree frogs produce much more of a chemical called photolyase, which repairs the damage ultra-violet light does to genes.

So ultra-violet light, let in by the damaged ozone layer, is killing frogs? There is only one problem with this story. There is no evidence of a decline in the thickness of the ozone layer over temperate latitudes; if anything there is more ozone about, made by car fumes. The temporary Antarctic and Arctic ozone 'holes' are thousands of miles away. So what's going on?

Closer inspection by the scientists revealed that there has been an epidemic of a fungus called *Saprolegnia* in frogs in the Pacific north-west. It seems to have spread from hatchery-reared trout and salmon. Perhaps the ultra-violet light is damaging the frog's ability to fight this new disease; such rays often do affect disease-fighting ability in other species. This may not have mattered until now, because the disease was not a problem. As yet we do not know.

In a sense, therefore, the ultra-violet light is indeed the problem. But in another sense, it may always have been a manageable problem and that has not changed. What has changed is the introduction of disease from fish farms. The real mystery, then, is why the western toads and Cascade frogs do not make as much photolyase as the Pacific tree frogs.

12. The Greenhouse Debate Must Stay on the Boil*

The greenhouse effect is about as solid a piece of science as exists. Carbon dioxide absorbs infra-red heat from the surface of the earth thus preventing it from escaping into space. Therefore the more carbon dioxide there is, the more the atmosphere grows warm. Right?

Well, according to a new scientific paper just published in a journal called *Spectrochimica Acta* by a respected scientist from Imperial College, maybe not right. Notice the gap in the logic of the first paragraph. Carbon dioxide may absorb heat, but it does not follow that more carbon dioxide absorbs more heat. After all, if you spill water on the floor and mop it up with a sponge, it does not matter how big the sponge is, it will not absorb more water than you spilled.

The same, according to Dr Jack Barrett, applies to carbon dioxide in the atmosphere. Imagine you are on a beam of infrared light of the right wavelength bouncing off the surface of the earth and heading for space. How far will you get before – for certain – hitting a carbon dioxide or water molecule and being absorbed? The answer turns out to be about ninety feet if you start at sea level. If there is more carbon dioxide in the air, you would get less far, and if less you would get a bit farther. But you would still get absorbed. The same amount of heat would therefore be trapped by more carbon dioxide.

Ah yes, say the greenhouse alarmists, but what happens then to the heat? It does not stay on board the carbon dioxide molecule, but is re-radiated as fluorescence (ie, a ray of a longer wavelength). The higher this fluorescence happens, the greater the chance the heat is lost in space. So more carbon dioxide means more heat does stay in the atmosphere.

Not so, says Dr Barrett. At low altitudes the carbon dioxide molecule is 10,000 times more likely to hit something than to

---

* Published in *The Sunday Telegraph* on 30 April 1995.

fluoresce, so it transfers its energy by collision, meaning the heat stays locally. Therefore, again, more carbon dioxide is like a bigger sponge used to mop up the same small spill. More carbon dioxide absorbs the same amount of heat.

Dr Barrett's paper is a reminder that not even the basic science of global warming theory can be considered beyond doubt. Despite much criticism, nobody has yet found a flaw in his logic. He is arguing that we can double the carbon dioxide in the atmosphere and it might not have any direct effect on climate. It might, but it might not.

A true scientist would respond to this by saying: this sounds like good news, but let us investigate it carefully and check it; if it turns out to be true, then we will breathe a sigh of relief because we need no longer suppress economic growth to save the planet. Instead, climatologists (most of whom are not trained in chemistry) have reacted like Jesuits to a new heresy. Suppress the news! Vilify the author! Stick to our guns! The truth is, they have such a vested interest in the climatic-change story that they can no longer be trusted to be objective.

I still believe that the balance of probability lies with the alarmists. More carbon dioxide will probably absorb more heat in the upper atmosphere, though not in the lower, the effects of clouds, dust and sunspots will probably not offset this effect and we will probably have a warmer climate a century hence because of all the fossil fuels we have been burning. But I do not consider the case closed and I am more and more disturbed by the McCarthyite way in which the debate is being conducted. Suppressing doubts is not the way to find the truth. The scientists and their environmental camp followers should treat us as grown-ups and air their arguments as well as their conclusions.

13. Why the Famine Forecasts are Wrong[*]

Famine is suddenly in the news again, not because it is happening, but because there has just been a conference in Washington on global food trends for the next quarter century. Such conferences are a time of plenty for alarmists, and sure enough a new alarmism is being spread abroad by Lester Brown of the Worldwatch Institute, which has been vainly predicting famine for years.

Brown's argument is that world grain stocks are lower than at any time since the early 1970s, that China is about to start importing large amounts of grain, as Russia did in the 1970s, and that, consequently, we are all going to starve. He has found willing megaphones in the media. Nor are farmers and grain traders averse to a spot of this alarmism; it keeps prices firm and justifies subsidies.

If Brown is right, is it not passing strange that America has taken large areas of land out of production, Europe has just followed suit and yet the world food price index is now one third of what it was in the mid-1970s? All the available evidence suggests that we are well within our capacity to feed the world population at present: famine deaths are at an all-time low, per-capita food production is at an all-time high and the price of wheat relative to wages is lower than ever before.

Such statistics do not satisfy Brown and his fellow alarmists. They maintain that the good news cannot last. The present revolution in agriculture is unsustainable, they say, because it depends on genetics, irrigation, fertilisers and pesticides. Geneticists will soon run out of ways to improve yields. Irrigation will soon run out of aquifers to tap. Fertilisers are made with finite supplies of oil. Pesticides are breeding resistance in pests.

---

[*] Published as 'Why the famine forecasts are hard to swallow' in *The Sunday Telegraph* on 18 June 1995.

Yet sustainability cuts both ways. Suppose that world farming used the same techniques as it did in the 1950s: before modern plant breeding, widespread irrigation, before pesticides and before cheap fertiliser. Suppose, in other words, we went organic. To produce the same amount of food as we now do, we would have to treble the acreage devoted to crop production, from 6 million to 16 million square miles.

This would be the equivalent of putting another North America under the plough. The effect on wildlife and habitat conservation would be drastic to say the least. There would be no room for the Serengeti, the Amazon or the Scottish Highlands: all would have to be cultivated. The plough would have to go into dry lands where soil erosion would destroy the ability of the land to recover. That's unsustainable.

It is a fact uncomfortable in the extreme to environmentalists, but the things that have done most to relieve the pressure on land, that have enabled us to afford nature reserves, that have prevented rain forests from far more destruction--are pesticides, fertilisers and higher-yielding plant varieties. The area of land under cultivation has increased by a mere 6 per cent in the past 40 years; the number of people to be fed has grown by 100 per cent in the same period, and the average person now has more to eat.

We in Britain may wish that our agriculture was less intensive (and less subsidised), so that there were more skylarks and butterflies on arable fields, but we can afford that luxury only because we can get dirt-cheap food from intensive agriculture all over the world. The distinction between farmland and wild land is growing ever starker, as farmland becomes more productive, monotonous and ugly, but at least that means the wild land can stay wild. The scientist working on a new and more deadly insecticide may not be the skylark's best friend, but he is actually doing more to save the rain forest than any number of campaigns against lavatory seats.

14. The Myth of Mystical Conservation*

I have been eavesdropping on an argument in anthropology. One side argues that indigenous people are 'natural' conservationists by virtue of their traditions and rituals. They are careful not to harvest or exploit any wild resource into extinction, and we can learn from their reverence for the environment. This is the side that dominates all television broadcasts about indigenous peoples and most newspaper articles; it is part of the essential public relations in favour of native people.

The other side argues that this is a romantic Rousseauian fantasy and that the only reason native people do not exterminate the local wildlife or exhaust the local resources is that they lack the technology or the demand to do so. Ritual exhortations to respect the environment are in practice meaningless. And to pretend otherwise is dangerous politics that has already begun to backfire.

There have now been three studies of Indians in the Amazon forest that have specifically tested the proposition that they are natural conservationists. For example, if Indians are natural conservationists they would spare pregnant female monkeys or those carrying babies. Instead they actively try to kill such animals because they are easier to catch. Likewise, when travelling through the depleted forest close to home en route to a distant hunt, they should pass up a chance to kill an animal they happen to see. In fact they always chase anything they come across, so long as it is big enough to be worth wasting a cartridge or an arrow on. They also readily use wasteful techniques like poisoning whole lakes to get a basketful of fish, or chopping down trees to get at the fruit.

Nor do taboos have any conservation effect at all. Indeed, as one anthropologist has pointed out, religion usually reinforces the tendency to overexploit resources. Shortages are blamed on

---

* Published as 'The savages hell-bent on destruction' in *The Sunday Telegraph* on 9 July 1995.

supernatural punishment, not overhunting. And, says another, venerating the prey is all very well, but the animal is no less dead for being venerated.

The strongest evidence for the revisionists comes from the waves of extinction that have followed hunters throughout the world in times past. We human beings wiped out over 70 per cent of the large mammalian genera in North America and 80 per cent of those in South America when we arrived 12,000 years ago, 100 per cent of the giant kangaroos in Australia 40,000 years ago, all of the moas of New Zealand, half of the birds of Hawaii and half of the lemurs of Madagascar.

There is now ample evidence that the North American Indians had all but exterminated elk, mule deer, bison and wolves from virtually all of the Rockies long before the white man started to help. Some conservationists!

The romantics now argue that even if it is untrue, the myth of the ecologically noble savage is valuable propaganda. The revisionists reply by citing the case of the Kayapo Indians, long revered for allegedly nurturing patches of forest, and now condemned as unusually 'bad Indians' for suddenly selling those forests to miners and loggers.

Yet there are clear cases in which the romantics are right. Local people do husband resources, at least until governments interfere. But these are cases not of religious taboos but of well-respected property rights enforced by sanctions. Indian bands 'owned' beaver lodges from which they trapped enough but not too many animals. Sulawesi people owned egg-laying sites of maleo birds. Fishing, grazing and irrigation rights were often carefully managed by systems of enforced local ownership, either by individuals or by families or communities. It was nationalisation of forests in India, of fisheries in Sri Lanka, of wildlife resources all over Africa that caused the free-for-all. Government is the problem, not the solution.

15. Can it be that We Need more Acid Rain?*

There are few more clear-cut success stories for environmentalists than the story of acid rain and forests. Trees began dying in Germany in the early 1980s. Scientists attributed the cause to sulphur dioxide in power-station smoke. Greens picked up the baton and with willing help from the press exaggerated the problem until it caught the ears of the politicians. New rules on sulphur emission were acrimoniously agreed by ministers. And by the early 1990s, coal-burning power stations were producing 30 per cent less sulphur dioxide than a decade before. The trees stopped dying.

It is a tidy tale of problem, diagnosis, action and cure to gladden the hearts of those who believe things can get better. Unfortunately, the emperor has no clothes on at all. There never was a problem, the diagnosis was wrong and the cure has done more harm than good. I say this not just with the benefit of hindsight, but with some *schadenfreude* because I was saying it at the time and nobody would listen. Now the facts are in.

Four years ago, at Liphook in Hampshire, an enormously expensive experiment began to test the effect of sulphuric acid and ozone on trees. Five plots of forest have been continuously fumigated with sulphur dioxide or ozone ever since to test the theory that these pollutants cause the trees to die. The results were unambiguous: the trees thrived.

There was, to quote the scientific report of the project, 'no evidence for universal forest decline symptoms'. Sitka spruce trees actually grew faster with sulphur dioxide. Ozone had no effect at all, thus badly denting the fallback theory of the German alarmists – that ozone weakens leaves, which acidity then damages.

So why were trees dying in the mid-1980s? Drought and pests, simple as that. In America, too, a giant official study came

---

* Published in *The Sunday Telegraph* on 15 October 1995.

to the same conclusion – there was no serious risk to forests from acid rain. But these studies came far too late to catch the news. The acid rain story, far from proving that government by pressure group works, is really quite a shocking example of how an environmental bandwagon once rolling, cannot be stopped. The facts no longer matter. What matters is that the public has had its mind made up for it.

Surely, though, it cannot have done any harm to cut out sulphur emissions from power plants, and might have done some good? After all, acid rain erodes statues and poisons lakes as well as ostensibly killing trees. Yes, but there are two reasons to pause before coming to this complacent conclusion. The first is that sulphur dioxide turns out to be an excellent chemical for reflecting sunlight back into space, and that it may therefore be good at delaying global warming, if that theory proves any more reliable than the acid rain theory.

Second, sulphur is now so scarce that plants are beginning to suffer for lack of it. Rape crops now need to have sulphur sprayed on them in many parts of the country or they succumb to disease of various kinds. Indeed, there is increasing evidence that trees, too, may be suffering from too little sulphur in the air. According to *New Scientist*, at least one German scientist, Dr Ewald Schnug of Brunswick, says sulphur compounds are good at neutralising the effect of ozone, which tends to weaken plants' defences against disease. By adding sulphur to the ground, he and his colleagues improved wheat yields by 20 per cent in one year.

Dr Schnug now blames the fact that trees are dying on the lack of sulphur dioxide in the air. Can it be long before the greens are clamouring for governments to show that they care for the environment by doing something about the disgraceful sulphur shortage in the atmosphere? How the world turns.

16. The Legend of Chief Seattle's Speech*

If there is anything approaching a sacred text in the environmental movement, it is a speech made by Chief Seattle of the Duamish Indians in 1855. So widely has this speech been used in books, films, children's teaching aids and sermons that there are now several subtly different versions of it in circulation. It was quoted at length by Albert Gore, Vice-President of the United States, in his best-seller, *Earth in the Balance*.

It is undoubtedly a moving speech: poetic, peaceable, wise and mystical. It shames us with our white, western values in its every cadence. Responding to an offer from the President of the United States to buy his land, the chief said, according to Gore's version:

'How can you buy or sell the sky? The land? The idea is strange to us...Every part of this earth is sacred to my people. Every shining pine needle, every sandy shore, every mist in the dark woods, every meadow, every humming insect. All are holy in the memory and experience of my people...Will you teach your children what we have taught our children? That the earth is our mother? What befalls the earth befalls all the sons of earth. This we know: the earth does not belong to man, man belongs to the earth. All things are connected like the blood that unites us all. Man does not weave the web of life, he is merely a strand in it. Whatever he does to the web, he does to himself.'

For a sixty-eight year old Indian slave-owner with a reputation for having killed many of his enemies and sold his land to whites, this was an extraordinarily prophetic statement of the central theme of deep ecology. Chief Seattle sounds just like a member of Greenpeace.

For years I have heard rumours that there is something wrong with the speech but it was not until I read a wonderful new book

---

* Published as 'Noble savage speaks with forked tongue' in *The Sunday Telegraph* on 22 October 1995.

44

by Stephen Budiansky, *Nature's Keepers* (Weidenfeld & Nicolson, £20), that I heard the whole truth.

To quote Budiansky: 'The reason Chief Seattle's speech sounded remarkably like the words of a twentieth-century, white, middle-class environmentalist was that they *were* the words of a twentieth-century, white, middle-class environmentalist.' They were written in 1971 for a fictional television programme by a man called Ted Perry.

There is only one record of what Chief Seattle said in 1855, a brief memory written down 30 years later by a white man who was there. According to this, Seattle merely praised the generosity of the president in buying his land. Perry simply put words into Seattle's mouth. He was writing fiction, and never pretended he was doing anything else.

The reason this is important is that Rousseau's myth of the 'noble savage' in tune with his environment in some holistic and paranormal way and immune to the capitalistic dictates of greed is a myth. There is no evidence for it at all. That is why environmentalists have latched on to fiction to support it.

When Daniel Day Lewis's screen father, Chingachgook, says to a deer his son has just killed, in the opening scene of the film *Last of the Mohicans*, 'We're sorry to kill you, brother. We do homage to your courage, speed and strength', it seems to our brainwashed imaginations like an authentic touch. But he was being anachronistic. There is little if any evidence that the 'thank-you-dead-animal' ritual was a part of Indian folklore before the twentieth century. Even if it was a common practice, the animal was no less dead, however much the killer apologised.

Indeed, the evidence that Indians had very nearly wiped out most of the big game – elk especially – in North America before the white men arrived is now incontrovertible. Mysticism only encouraged such despoliation of the environment by blaming gods, not people, for any shortage of game.

45

17. Reassuring Facts about BSE*

Tucking into a lamb stir-fry the other night I was struck by a sudden thought. People are avoiding beef because of mad-cow disease. But where did the cows get the disease in the first place? From eating the brains of sheep infected with the disease scrapie. So people ought to be avoiding lamb as well.

Before I get hate mail from hill farmers all over the country, let me hasten to add that I do not think anybody should avoid either. The chances of mad-cow disease infecting human beings with Creutzfeldt-Jakob disease are very small. I say this not with the false-reassuring condescension government experts prefer, but because of having read a bit about the thing that causes the disease.

I say 'thing', because it is truly the most remarkable disease on the planet: the only infectious disease that is also hereditary, and the only infectious disease that has no genes. It is just a molecule that has the odd property of turning normal molecules into itself. When Stanley Prusiner first discovered this in the 1970s nobody would believe him, but he has persisted and been proved right.

Excuse a brief technical diversion. We all have the prion protein molecule in every one of our nerve cells. We could not exist without it. But sometimes, usually because of an inherited mutation, one prion takes on a wrong shape as two of its spiral staircases unravel. There is no chemical change, just a change in shape. When this happens the new shaped prion (known as a scrapie prion) goes round turning ordinary prions into the same shape as itself. They in turn go round transforming other prions until the whole brain is affected.

A scrapie prion ingested by eating an infected animal can start a similar cascade of unravelling in the consuming animal. This is what happened in New Guinea, where the Fore people caught the

---

* Published as 'My beef with the mad cow scaremongers' in *The Sunday Telegraph* on 19 November 1995.

disease kuru from eating the brains of their dead relatives, and in Britain where cattle caught it from eating the brains of scrapie-infected sheep.

But – and here's the one piece of comfort in all this – altered prions from one species cannot necessarily transform those of another. The more distantly related the species, the more differences there are between their prions. There are in total 254 building blocks in each prion. In sheep and cattle just seven of those are different – and cattle can get the disease from sheep. Between mice and hamsters there are 16 differences and mice cannot normally get the disease from hamsters.

Between human beings and cattle, there are 30 differences, which is deeply reassuring – the species barrier is almost twice as high as between hamsters and mice, where it is just about high enough.

I suspect the recent (tiny) spate of cases of Creutzfeldt-Jakob disease reflects more frequent diagnosis. Depression and dementia have always happened. Only recently have people begun to attribute some of it to prion disease.

The perils of spurious trends caused by better diagnosis was reinforced last week by Professor Sam Shuster, who argued in *The Lancet* that far more melanomas are now diagnosed than before, many of them falsely, because of the scares about sunlight. This in turn inflates the statistics, which increases the scares about sunlight and so on round the vicious circle. The evidence linking melanomas to sunlight is actually poor. For example, many melanomas appear on parts of the skin least exposed to sunlight. The evidence linking the much more common benign forms of skin cancer to sunlight is far greater, and some doctors and environmentalists deliberately blur the distinction between them to disguise the weakness of the case against sunlight.

18. Man's Meat, Woman's Veg*

As 1995 ended, world wheat prices were at a 14-year high, stocks were at a 20-year low and China was for the first time importing large quantities of grain. For those of a pessimistic turn of mind, this looks ominous. Is population at last catching up with food production? Is the green revolution ending and a new era of famine beginning?

In fact, the outlook for feeding the 12 billion-15 billion people expected to inhabit the globe by the end of the next century has never looked brighter. World food production per head is rising as fast as ever, thanks to steadily improving yields: it now stands at 140 per cent of 1950 levels. The price of grain is one-third of what it was 100 years ago in real terms, and one-tenth when indexed by average wages.

So comfortably is the world feeding itself that not only will Europe again set aside 8-12 per cent of its arable land as fallow next year and America 36m acres, but they will each feed about two-thirds of their grain to animals to make meat out of it. This wastes about 90 per cent of the calories along the way. The amount of meat, especially chicken and pork, eaten by the people of the world is growing steadily. In 1996 the world will consume more than 75m tonnes of pork, much more than the tonnage of beef, lamb and goat combined.

1996 will see the inevitable crop of scaremongering reports about imminent famines. Remember when you hear them that we not only feed 100 per cent more people on just 6 per cent more land than we did 40 years ago, but that we also devote most of that land to growing food for our domestic animals, rather than ourselves.

Indeed, the whole reason for China's new hunger for imported grain is to be found not in its imminent starvation but in its swelling, carnivorous prosperity. The Chinese appetite for pork

---

* Published in *The World in 1996* by © The Economist Publications.

is up by one-third in just five years, while the amount of beef eaten per head has more than doubled in the same period. Meanwhile, across the Eurasian landmass, the British and the Germans, more than any other nations, are turning away from meat, out of a mixture of concern for animal rights and health-consciousness. Although the Americans have slightly increased their consumption of beef and pork during the 1990s, in Britain and Germany the consumption of both is falling steeply. In Britain the welfare and rights of farm animals are rapidly becoming an explosive moral and political issue marked by irreconcilable differences, martyrs and violence.

Such a political snowball can only grow. From decrying the fur trade, the campaigners moved on to the export of veal calves; expect them next to attack dairy farms and chicken batteries, the most egregious cases of animals treated cruelly on farms. Such protests could soon be among Britain's leading exports. Germans will follow suit, just as green issues from anti-nuclear protests to acid-rain scare stories spread west from Germany to Britain in the 1980s.

Strict vegetarians were roughly as numerous in Britain as homosexuals ten years ago; now they are three times as common. But whereas homosexuals are mostly men, roughly twice as many women as men are vegetarian, a difference that is probably as old as the stone age, when men hunted meat while women gathered vegetables.

The young are the shock troops of vegetarianism. According to one survey, 24 per cent of British women between 18 and 24 are vegetarians, up from 8 per cent in 1984. Eight-year-old London girls now demand Linda McCartney's branded vegetarian sausages from their friends' mothers at tea parties. Not all of this is ideological. Mad-cow disease and cholesterol-phobia have something to do with it as well. But many women, especially in their semi-anorexic teens, simply dislike meat. Nowadays, moreover, they can get a much greater range of protein-rich fresh vegetables than was the case a decade ago. There is less risk of beri-beri.

This is because food is being liberated from all taint of geography and season. Europeans eat South African avocados in winter and there is no longer such a thing as the strawberry season. Increasingly, each country's agriculture can abandon the growing of staple food and exploit its comparative advantages instead. The Kenyan peasant will grow out-of-season *mangestout* peas which he can sell for more Iowa maize and Danish bacon then he could ever grow himself. As in industry, specialisation is the path of the future. Only backward-looking governments, such as the European Commission, still preach self-sufficiency in all crops and meats – a prejudice worse than any vegetarian's.

19. The Sixth Extinction*

The Sixth Extinction: Biodiversity and its Survival, by Richard Leakey and Roger Lewin (Weidenfeld & Nicolson, 288pp, £18.99)

On most computers there is a button called 'reset' that clears the screen and starts all over again, wiping out whatever is in the memory at the time. You can start afresh, unburdened by the clutter of the recent past. (Desks should have reset buttons.)

The planet Earth has a reset button, called mass extinction. It has been pressed five times so far. The most drastic occasion was at the end of the Permian period, 225 million years ago, when 95 per cent of all marine animal species became extinct. It has been pressed twice since, most recently 65 million years ago, when the finger that punched it was an errant comet that struck Mexico with the force of a billion Hiroshimas. The result was a lot of dead dinosaurs.

But mass extinctions are opportunities as well as ends. The Permian wipe-out gave the molluscs their lucky break to take over from their rivals, the brachiopods. The death of the dinosaurs was the opportunity for which our ancestors, the mammals, had been waiting tens of millions of years.

And according to Richard Leakey and Roger Lewin (not that they use my analogy), the finger is now poised over the button again, and this time it is a human finger. We are wiping out species at such a rate that our successors will look back and wonder what hit the planet.

It is not an original idea. Indeed, biodiversity experts vying with each other for new ways to catch our attention (and our wallets) first hit on the notion of a 'sixth mass extinction' some years ago. But Leakey is well placed to expand on it, being both the world's most famous fossil expert and the world's most famous elephant saviour. He has teamed up again with Roger

---

* Published as 'Nowhere to go' in *Literary Review* in February 1996.

Lewin, who has ghostwritten some of his previous books, to pull together three rather different stories: the history of life on earth, the ecology of complex communities of species, and the extinguishing effect of man. It is a strange tale, well told and with well-chosen examples.

The book is full of fascinating controversies. What caused the big mass extinctions? What wiped out the mammoths? How big is the current mass extinction? How do you save the elephant? On every controversy, Leakey and Lewin give us a nice flavour of the debate – and then hedge their bets. Meteorites cause mass extinctions, except sometimes when volcanoes or sea-level changes might. The current mass extinction is big, but perhaps not as big as the 100,000 species a year estimated by some alarmists. People wiped out mammoths, but perhaps the climate played a role. Legal protection will save the elephant, but Leakey (the book is written in the first person) is not against sustainable use of them. I was occasionally left muttering: 'Make up your mind.'

There is no doubt that there has been a mass extinction of large mammals and birds since the last ice age, and that we are responsible. Within a few hundred years of human arrival many of the larger animals of North and South America, Australia, Madagascar, New Guinea, New Zealand and the islands of the Pacific and Indian Oceans had disappeared. This adds up to quite a list: dodos, moas, diprotodons, passenger pigeons, giant armadillos – in all perhaps 20 per cent or more of all mammals and birds.

But far from being a warning to us, Stone Age extinctions are not a good guide to what is going on now. In every case, the fauna was naïve. It did not know and did not learn quickly enough that humans should be run away from. We have been noticeably less effective in wiping out the animals of our native continent, Africa, precisely because we have been there so long. And most of the species were on islands.

Islands and lakes are the places most vulnerable to extinction, because they have unique faunas with nowhere to go. Take birds. We have wiped out about 20 per cent of bird species. But nearly all of those – with just a handful of exceptions – were on remote islands. It has proved remarkably difficult to kill off continental tropical birds. In Brazil, for instance, 90 per cent of the coastal rain forest has gone and not a single endemic bird has died out.

Islands take away, and islands give. Stranded on islands, in lakes, on mountain tops or in fragments of isolated forest or even in national parks, species diverge into new species. Fragmentation is vital to speciation, and mankind is supremely good at fragmenting habitat. We have almost certainly dramatically increased the speciation rate as well as the extinction rate.

These thoughts are not much consolation to those who would like to have seen a dodo or a passenger pigeon, or who lament the many beetles as yet undescribed by science now disappearing in the Amazon forest. But they are more interesting than the futile debate about how many species are actually becoming extinct at present. Ecologists have described a million species, which could be 1 per cent or 10 per cent of the total. They are recording the extinction of a few, which could be 1 per cent or 10 per cent of the total. This gives figures for annual extinction rates of between 100 and 100,000 species. It is the purest and silliest guesswork.

Instead, the book provides a much more interesting and significant number: the proportion of the world's primary productivity (a posh term for plants) that now flows through human bodies as opposed to animal. According to Leakey's sources, this could be as high as 40 per cent: four out of every ten calories of sunlight absorbed by the biosphere are consumed by humanity. Even if this is a gross overestimate, which it must be, it emphasises the scale of the problem. We cannot ask all the other species on the planet to move over to make room for our monocultures of wheat and timber without expecting some of them to fall out the other side of the bed.

That is the inexorable reason for the current mass extinction. Lamenting it is too easy. What this reader longs to know is, if Richard Leakey were world dictator, how would he stop it? Suppose his re-election depended on how many species he saved (he has recently, and with much courage, entered Kenyan politics).

The answer lies in the rain forests, because they have by far the largest number of species. Repealing the facts of economics (or worse, as this book does, blaming economists for them) would achieve nothing. The more intensively we industrialise and farm the rest of the planet, and the lower we drive timber prices, the less pressure there is on rain forests.

Or ask yourself why it is that a man chops down a forest when its present net value in sustainable crops is six times greater standing. He does it because he cannot monopolise the sustainable revenue, but he can monopolise the timber revenue. The key, in other words, is ownership. If Leakey and Lewin are right, and rain forests really are worth more standing than felled, the answer is easy: privatise them by granting them acre by acre to individual Indians, and the new owners will look after them. That is where the logic leads.

20. The Cold Truth about Global Warming*

The Global Warming Debate, ed. by John Emsley (The European Science and Environment Forum, £15)

The Earth's climate is getting hotter. Man-made carbon dioxide is the main cause. The rate of warming is predicted to be faster than at any time in history. Computer models accurately mimic world climate. The effect of climate change on the ecology of the planet will be disastrous. Virtually all reputable scientists agree with all these sentences.

All of the sentences in the preceding paragraph are false. This book – a series of essays (some brilliant, some terrible) by scientists dissenting from the alarmist consensus on global warming – proves as much in painstaking and convincing detail.

There is no current warming trend at all, according to reliable balloon and satellite data. Man-made carbon dioxide is not the main cause of atmospheric warming: at most it amounts to four per cent of natural effects. Even the official models now predict as little as half a degree of warming in the next century – which will be all but undetectable. The computer models of the world's climate are hopelessly poor predictive tools, made to fit past data only by heroic feats of fudging.

The official predictions about the effects of global warming produce mixed results – just as many positive as negative ones. But the positive ones are suppressed. And the great 'consensus' among scientists on this matter is a piece of circular argument: only those scientists who agree with the conventional wisdom are allowed to influence the papers put out by the United Nations.

The truth is, catastrophic man-made global warming is no longer likely. It was a hypothesis, based on plausible but flawed physics, that has not stood up to scrutiny. Global warming is, in fact, either going to be mild or non-detectable against the normal

---

* Published in *The Sunday Telegraph* on 17 March 1996.

fluctuations of climate. Yet too many people now have a vested interest in it to admit as much.

The 'Greenhouse' industry is a splendid gravy train providing luxurious jobs for bureaucrats (the three-year 'Global Environment Facility' set up at the Rio summit in 1992 has just quietly made itself permanent), lavish grants for scientists, lashings of publicity for Green pressure groups, and a steady supply of alarmist stories for journalists with which to catch editors' attention.

So all these groups are defending alarmism for all they are worth, and using some questionable tactics to boot, as this book reveals: one scientist refused to release details of his data to a scientist appointed by the United Nations to review it.

The Global Warming Debate is a devastating exercise in imperial strip-tease. The many scientists who contributed to it are not prepared to go on telling the emperor he is fully clothed.

The European Science and Environment Forum: 73 McCarthy Court, London, SW11 3ET, UK

21. Too Soon – and Too Late – to Panic over BSE[*]

Yesterday's announcement that 10 people may (just may) have caught dementia from eating meat, rather than inherited their illness in the human form, has rather overshadowed the fact that this is Science Week. Yet the two facts are connected.

The Government's difficulty, both in understanding the disease in question and in reassuring people, comes down to a very basic issue of science. The thing that causes Creutzfeldt-Jakob disease and mad cow disease is a very mysterious creature. Scientists knew very little about it when they started and they know not much more now. As a result, they have made mistakes.

When I first wrote about scrapie (the sheep version of the disease) in the mid-1980s I was assured by British scientists that it was a virus. They distrusted a new theory coming from California that scrapie was the only disease organism on the planet that had no genes; that it was an infectious protein molecule. We now know that the Californian Stanley Prusiner was right. Scrapie, kuru, CJD, FFI and BSE – they are all caused by a molecule that Prusiner called a prion. It has no DNA, the stuff of genes, and it is smaller than the smallest virus.

Why does such an arcane detail matter? For this reason: if scrapie had indeed been a virus, we would have quickly known a good deal about it – how you catch it, how you avoid it, whether you can vaccinate against it, how long its incubation period is and which species of animal it infected. Instead, the thing has kept on surprising us. Unlike all other diseases, it can be both infectious and heritable. The medics, used to dealing with viruses, were groping in the dark for a long time with scrapie.

This simple distinction, between viruses and prions, is not at all hard to understand. But scientists, journalists and politicians

[*] Published as 'Too soon to panic over BSE' in *The Daily Telegraph* on 21 March 1996

57

are all united in their determined belief that people are incapable of handling simple scientific facts. So none of them ever even attempts this explanation and the debate remains serenely speculative – and therefore scary. If a minister says beef is safe, and somebody else says it is not, we have no way of knowing which to believe unless we have some facts.

We now know quite a lot about prions. They live in brains and are simply an altered form of perfectly normal molecules we all have therein. We know you can inherit them in your genes, get them by transplants from infected pituitary glands, and get them by eating the brains of dead relatives (which happened in New Guinea in the 1950s), and we know that animals can catch them from other animals. So much for the bad news.

We also know some reassuring things. The more closely related two animals are, the more easily they catch prions from each other. Cows can catch them from sheep quite easily – which is how BSE started – but hamsters can catch them from mice only with difficulty. Therefore, if human beings can catch them from cattle, then they will do so only rarely, probably very rarely indeed. The fact that only 10 potential cases have come to light in a population of tens of millions of people who ate beef between 1986 and 1989 is consistent with that.

We know also that the risk is largely in the past, centred on the four years during which sheep offal was fed, undercooked, to cattle: 1986-1989. The number of cases of BSE peaked about five years later and is now falling. The human problem, if it appears, will therefore not yet have peaked, but new cases of infection caused by beef eaten today are most unlikely.

Moreover, almost all the cases of BSE have appeared in dairy herds, and most of the dangerous feed was fed to dairy cattle. So beef, which comes from beef cattle of different breeds, is almost certainly safer than the figures would imply. (Conversely, having eaten lamb in the dangerous years is no consolation, for scrapie started in sheep.) But you have to eat part of the brain to run any risk at all. Steaks and milk are much safer.

All this leads me to stick to my view that an epidemic of human BSE is completely out of the question, and that no cases at all is still the most likely outcome. But a few human cases in the years to come is still a possibility. Government, caught between wanting to avoid scaring people (and thereby damaging farmers' livelihoods) and knowing too little to be categorical about anything, has left many people convinced that there has been a conspiracy to cover up alarming facts. As usual, the conspiracy theory is far less convincing than the cock-up theory. This disease is too little known for categorical declarations – either way.

PART III

SUITS AND SANDALS: PUBLIC CHOICE AND THE ENVIRONMENT

22. The Revolt Against Subsidised Forestry*

In the Scottish border hills, from Galloway across to the Cheviots, something is stirring: a popular revolt against a hated invader. It is an environmental rebellion, but not of the kind orchestrated by self-seeking activists in London offices; it comes from the genuine grass roots.

The invader is sitka spruce. Borderers are not anti-forestry – indeed most want more trees – but they are increasingly upset by the manner in which their hills are being lost under the jackroot of the blue, Alaskan tyrant. Shepherds' jobs vanish, shops and schools close, open landscape is lost and silence falls for 40 years until the chainsaw heralds either a pathetically small return, or just as likely the wind blows the whole lot down.

The reason this is happening is that the Forestry Commission, egged on by Greens, is hellbent on achieving a 'target' of 33,000 hectares of new forestry planting a year and the border hills are the most promising place to do it. Land is cheaper than in England and the environmentalists less active than in the Highlands.

The Forestry Commission is not itself planting much new land. But it approves planting grants to private companies, particularly the two giant commercial foresters, Tilhill and Fountain. These grants have replaced the tax breaks that encouraged so many pop stars to plant trees in the 1980s.

Every economic decision in the uplands is governed by subsidies. There are really only three competitive uses for hill land: subsidised sheep farming, subsidised tree planting and unsubsidised grouse shooting. Of the three, forestry is the option locals least like, but the one that usually values the land highest. It does so not because there is demand for its competitive products – short-rotation, tropical pulp timber makes a mockery

---

* Published as 'Borders at bay in roots and branch revolt' in *The Sunday Telegraph* on 20 November 1994.

of Scottish sitka costs – but because the planting is directly and generously subsidised.

Fifty years ago, when commercial forestry first began blanketing the hills with square green rugs, it seemed to promise jobs – harvesting and processing the timber. The promise was broken. Harvesting is now so mechanised that machines eat whole trees. Processing is non-existent, because bad silvicultural practice – planting shallow rooted trees on wet soils, then not daring to thin them lest they blow – has left a crop only suitable for cheap pulp, not timber. The only timber-related industry that thrives is haulage.

The Campaign for the Border Hills argues that subsidies should be adjusted so that they encourage a mixture of sheep farming and small areas of tree planting, rather than losing whole farms to sitka spruce. This is not hard to arrange by limiting grants to small woodlands or allowing planting costs to be set against genuine farming profits before tax. But it may never happen because the 'forestry lobby' consists of two commercial firms in a cosy alliance with one all powerful nationalised industry that also acts as judge and jury of all planting applications: the Forestry Commission. It even picks the lay members of Regional Advisory Committees who represent local interests on planting applications.

True, the commission has begun to make its own forests nicer to look at. Computer simulations now show you how the great Kielder monoculture will look once the valleys are clothed in broad-leaved trees and the clear-felled areas are small, irregular and 'natural'. All this is welcome and imaginative. But before you express too much gratitude, remember you the taxpayer are paying for this, and it would have been nice had they asked you what you wanted decades ago, or even if they did so now. As usual public ownership effectively means ownership by public employees, not by the public.

23. Buying Land is a Waste of Lottery Money*

The national lottery is about to deliver a great windfall for conservation. A deluge of lottery money, perhaps £30 million a year, could now be spent by the National Heritage Memorial Fund on environmental projects alone. But I fear that much of the money could be spent on the purchase of land – which in itself does nothing to improve the environment. Unless the fund is careful – and I believe they will be – the lottery could accelerate the nationalisation of the countryside.

The fund cannot solicit applications, can only countenance capital projects and will only give money to charitable organisations and public bodies. This means that the best organised and most acquisitive charities, such as the National Trust and the Royal Society for the Protection of Birds, may end up with the lion's share, and they will, I confidently predict, use the money to 'save' sites that come up for sale. For which read acquire them for themselves.

Take the case of the Scottish highlands. At present if a big highland estate comes on the market, three kinds of creature compete to buy it: spendthrift millionaires, conservation bodies and corporate investors such as pension funds. Until Sir Hector Munro, minister in the Scottish Office, recently stopped the practice, the conservation bodies were actually getting a taxpayers' subsidy for their bids. Sir Hector was right. If the RSPB or the John Muir Trust wants to own an estate, let it ask its members or the public for the money directly, and if they won't produce it then they don't want it badly enough. Why should the poor old taxpayer pick up the bill?

However, the poor old lottery player could now do so instead. This risks bidding up the price of land and rewarding rich vendors. It does precisely nothing to preserve or improve the

---

* Published as 'Lottery cash can save the country's face' in *The Sunday Telegraph* on 27 November 1994.

65

landscape. It does not even prevent competing buyers from turning the land into a theme park, because the planning laws already prevent that, whoever owns it. It does not even secure public access, which is available on private Scottish mountains anyway. Buying land achieves nothing in itself. Not one tree is planted, not one corncrake encouraged. It is just the state relieving a rich person of the burden of subsidising the land's capital and running costs and handing them to the public instead.

The National Heritage Memorial Fund does require the recipient to have a detailed conservation management plan before it will fund them and will in exceptional circumstances fund an endowment. But it can do little if the only applications it gets are for land purchase. I hope the big charities will recognise this, suppress their hunger for land ownership and instead dream up imaginative projects under which the money would not buy land but improve it. Plant a forest, restore heather to an overgrazed hill, turn an arable field into a wood, undo a drainage system – such things cost money and provide jobs.

For example, the River Garry upstream of Blair Atholl in Perthshire was a canoeists', anglers' and dipper's paradise until the 1950s when the government in its wisdom built a hydroelectric scheme that takes all the water out at the top of the valley, sends it down a pipe and puts it back in at the bottom. The river bed has been as dry as a desert creek ever since, a disgrace to the government that killed it. So why not use the lottery money to put the river back: blow up the dams, build a little gas-fired power station to replace the electricity output of the hydro scheme and give the public somewhere to play?

It is better to spend money improving the bad bits of the countryside than changing the ownership of the good bits.

24. Who Speaks for the Yanomamo?*

A war of words (and worse) is being waged in the forests of Venezuela. The protagonists all claim to have at heart the interests of the Yanomamo people, the most famous of the Amazonian native Indians, who are the only people in the argument not being heard from. They are being fought over by two rival camps of anthropologists, a church of religious missionaries, two rival environmental groups and assorted politicians.

At the centre of the argument is the man who put the Yanomamo on the map 30 years ago, an American anthropologist called Napoleon Chagnon. He began to study them in the 1960s, wrote a best-selling book about them (originally called *Yanomamo: the fierce people*, politically corrected in the latest edition to *Yanomamo: the last days of Eden*) and then fell out with his fellow anthropologists because he described Yanomamo society with all its warts, including the central role played by war, feuds and sexual competition. This did not fit with Rousseauian ideas of noble savages then coming into fashion in anthropology.

He also fell out with the Roman Catholic Salesian missionaries in the area, whom he accused of (until 1991) bribing the Indians with shotguns and outboard motors, which made their wars more bloody, and attracting them into settlements where they die of disease at three times the rate of remote villages. The Salesians, joined by Mr Chagnon's anthropological enemies and the various survival groups busy promoting the Yanomamo as environmental saints, replied with vitriolic character assassinations of Mr Chagnon and his Venezuelan collaborator, Charles Brewer-Carias, a former minister, whom they accused of being in league with rapacious gold miners called *garimpeiros*.

---

* Published as 'Noble savages caught up in forest crossfire' in *The Sunday Telegraph* on 4 December 1994.

'What you need is some psychotherapy. Your state of paranoia disturbs me,' wrote one French anthropologist in an open letter forwarded by the Salesians to grant-giving bodies in America to poison them against Mr Chagnon.

Matters came to a head in September 1993 when a group of Brazilian *garimpeiros* massacred a whole band of Yanomamos including women and children. The Venezuelan president appointed a commission to investigate, naming both Mr Chagnon and Mr Brewer to it, but on arrival it was bundled unceremoniously off the site by a rival commission organised by another branch of the government more friendly to the Salesians. Mr Chagnon says the Salesians are anxious to protect evidence of their past complicity in violence; the Salesians say Mr Chagnon's commission was annulled five days after it was created; Mr Chagnon says it was not.

The argument now burns in the pages of anthropology journals, where increasingly long lists of increasingly distinguished academics either attack or defend Mr Chagnon. The murdering *garimpeiros* remain unpunished.

It is, at bottom, a debate about ownership. The Salesians were granted a large measure of secular authority over the Amazonian Indians in 1915 and this is threatened by the creation of a state of Amazonas in 1992. Mr Chagnon is likewise accused by fellow anthropologists of jealously guarding his reputation as Mr Yanomamo against rival expertise.

The starring role thrust upon the Yanomamo people as rain forest inhabitants during the Rio environmental summit has now led to a new ownership war between two environmental organisations, Survival International in London and Cultural Survival in Boston. Each claims to be the true representative of the Indians (though both vilify Mr Chagnon for his Hobbesian line). Mud is flying.

The Indians, meanwhile, do their best to suffer in silence and retain their dignity amid this playground squabbling.

25. The Tragedy of the Commons*

'The tragedy of the commons' is economists' shorthand for the fact that nobody looks after resources held in common. It is a truth borne out by the state of common-pool properties all over the world, from herring fisheries to bus shelters. But it is a lesson people seem immune to learning.

Garrett Hardin, an American economist, coined the phrase after studying the overgrazing of medieval English commons: the benefit of every extra cow was captured by the cow's owner; the cost of overgrazing was shared with all users of the common. No more perfect illustration of this exists than Bodmin moor in Cornwall, where 23 separate grazing commons exist, shared between the cattle and sheep of those who own the inalienable rights to graze them. The moor is overgrazed, and nobody can do anything about it because a commoner who cuts down his stock numbers merely benefits another less responsible neighbour.

Three years ago the commoners and landowners decided to mend the tragedy. They got Cornwall County Council to promote a private Bill in Parliament to create a Commmoners' Council with power to restrict grazing. The Ministry of Agriculture said that if the council did so, it would reward the moor with the status of an Environmentally Sensitive Area, and generous grants would follow. Grazing would be reduced, to the benefit of plants and animals, but farmers would be better off; everybody would be happy.

All went well until this year, when the Countryside Commission weighed in on behalf of the Ramblers and the Open Spaces Society. It demanded that the Bill include statutory public access to the common. The promoters refused and have now threatened to withdraw the Bill if Parliament obeys the Countryside Commission and makes public access statutory. That would be back to square one: overgrazing and all. The

---

* Published as 'The moor that cries out for a common touch' in *The Sunday Telegraph* on 18 December 1994.

69

Countryside Commission would have been responsible for preventing improvement of both the countryside and those who live in it.

But surely this is obstinacy on the part of the commoners? Surely public access to Bodmin moor is harmless? Yes: at present there is free access to most of the moor most of the time for anybody who wants to go there, and the bill would not change that at all. But it is permissive, not statutory access; landowners could prevent it but do not. This sort of arrangement exists all over the country from woods in the home counties to hills in Wales. It works well, and it leaves in place the landowner's right to throw off vandals, badger baiters and those who cannot control their dogs while giving unhindered access to the peaceable.

At Bodmin the Countryside Commission seems dedicated to pursuing a different and entirely foreign form of access – a statutory 'right to roam' – in which all powers to protect that land are confiscated from the person responsible for the land and he becomes a second-class citizen on his own property. Even if they believe such a policy is right nationally, the commissioners have no business hijacking somebody else's environmental bill to pursue their agenda.

As many cases have exemplified, a statutory right to roam produces in short order a tragedy of the commons. Nobody any longer has any interest in looking after the land. Why protect badger setts in a place where anybody can go unchallenged? Why pick up litter? Why plant trees? Those who do none of these things merely reap the rewards of those who do them. Bodmin does not deserve to be punished for being a model of successful, permissive public access. Statutory public access, by contrast, is the fast route to environmental ruin.

26. Bureaucrats Who Maximise
their Budgets*

The government's plan to create an Environment Agency, laid out in a bill published before Christmas, has met with virtually no opposition. That fact alone makes me suspicious.

The Environment Agency – a 9,000-bureaucrat, overhead camshaft, *premier cru* new quango – would replace and absorb two national quangos, the National Rivers Authority and Her Majesty's Inspectorate of Pollution, as well as taking over the waste-regulation functions of county councils. In the House of Lords, where the bill to create it first appeared, speaker after speaker praised the idea. One-stop shop, they said, makes sense, tidies up the situation, gives environmental protection some teeth, and so on.

There was one minor flurry of excitement when some hawk-eyed Green spotted that the new agency would not, like the present NRA, have a 'duty to further pollution control' in the long list of duties spelt out in its terms of reference, and suspected that this was an attempt to weaken its powers. Indeed, one NRA bureaucrat even lobbied me at a public meeting on this matter, painting a picture of devious ministers neutering his powers to create work for himself. My joy at this prospect was short-lived. The government has admitted that such had not been their intention at all; indeed their wording had been intended to widen, not narrow the powers of the new agency.

When pressure groups and opposition parties find so little wrong with something, my eyebrows rise. The Child Support Agency, after all, and the Dangerous Dogs Bill were greeted with similar universal nodding. I have a nasty feeling that you will be hearing more about the Environment Agency in years to come.

---

* Published as 'The green baby waiting to grow into a monster' in *The Sunday Telegraph* on 8 January 1995.

71

The principal problem is centralisation. Although the NRA has achieved a vast improvement in the control of water pollution since its creation in 1989, it was only making up for the incompetence and corruption of its predecessors. As Roger Bate of the Institute of Economic Affairs has shown, nationalising the problem of pollution created a polluters' charter, because it protected them from common law. In the 1950s, anglers' organisations brought a growing number of successful actions against river polluters (the best example being the Pride of Derby case in 1953). But common law rights of anglers and landowners then became secondary to statutory authority, and most polluters are therefore effectively protected from civil action by their statutory duties not to exceed limits and so on. They can be criminally prosecuted for excess pollution, but not sued under civil law for 'normal' pollution. They therefore have no incentive to improve.

For example, last year salmon died in large numbers in the lower reaches of the river Tyne. Anglers upstream and riparian owners who invest in fishing can do nothing about it, because the polluter has a permit to pollute. The Tyne no longer cleans itself out in spates, because of the dam of Kielder reservoir; in summer when river levels are kept low by Northumbrian Water, the pollution matters disproportionately more.

One riparian owner did at least win a moral victory over the NRA, though. He sent them a sample of the river bed algal sludge formed by the lack of spates and told them it came from a polluted stream. They were down in force in a flash to inspect this stream, and much embarrassed to be told it was the main river itself.

I hope I shall be proved wrong and the Environment Agency will be a force against pollution, rather than a force for growing its own budget. But precedents are not encouraging. Once the responsibility for something trickles up to Whitehall, we all know what happens to accountability. It vanishes. *Vide* the prison service.

27. Danger: Wildlife at Risk from the Do-gooders*

Animal welfare is getting in the way of conservation. Good conservation does not just mean protecting habitats. It also means managing ecosystems for maximum diversity and that often means controlling some species. Most conservation organisations know this and even practise it. But they dare not say so for fear of offending the animal-welfarists among their members.

This is what makes next month's Commons debate on fox hunting so other-worldly. Everybody knows that fox hunting encourages foxes; without it they would be far more cruelly and frequently persecuted. Ironically, that might be good for the creatures they prey upon, so rabbit lovers should be in favour of the Bill, but fox lovers should be against it.

Likewise, it still suits the Royal Society for the Protection of Birds to persecute gamekeepers at every opportunity. They not only do the police's work in gathering evidence to prosecute those who kill birds of prey (and not a few who do not); they also frequently blacken the whole profession with the charge.

Since gamekeepers drove most hawks to the brink of extinction a century or so ago, and some undoubtedly still flout the law, this is an understandable reaction. I even suspect that some of the dangers hawks pose to game are a bit exaggerated; goshawks, for example, kill crows, which are great persecutors of gamebirds' nests. What I object to is the fact that conservationists steadfastly refuse to acknowledge that, on balance, gamekeepers do more good than harm for conservation.

For a start, most birds of prey are not in trouble. The peregrine, harrier, goshawk and sparrowhawk – chief targets of gamekeepers – are increasing not just gradually, but fast; they are approaching saturation in many areas. The merlin and barn owl, with which gamekeepers have no argument, are in trouble.

---

* Published in *The Sunday Telegraph* on 19 February 1995.

Nor is cruelty the issue. The RSPB cannot object to killing when it does some itself. It kills crows, the most intelligent of birds, to protect rarities in some of its reserves. It is party to something called the Ruddy Duck Working Group, which sent me a press release recently about testing 'the effectiveness of shooting ruddy ducks with shotguns'. (It depends, they will find, on the aim.)

Meanwhile, unsung, gamekeepers do more for the conservation of some declining species than any number of nature reserves. Dr Peter Garson of Newcastle University has shown a close correlation between the lack of crows and the number of breeding curlews, lapwings and black grouse in the north Pennines and Cheviots – all three are declining species. The more gamekeepers there are in an area, the fewer crows and the more lapwings.

A new paper on moorland from Scottish Natural Heritage, English Nature and the Joint Nature Conservation Committee admits that gamekeepers are good for conservation. Without the economic rationale they represent, it says, moorland birds and moorland itself would decline.

Conservationists hate saying this out loud, because most of their members are motivated not by conservation, but by animal welfare; moral outrage generates more cheques. Yet animal-welfare squeamishness is not the only reason for this hesitancy. Most conservationists still subscribe to the Panglossian school of ecology that was fashionable in the 1970s – that nature always creates a balance and all is for the best in the best of all possible worlds. Crows must be all right because they are part of nature. Modern scientific ecologists have abandoned such a view. Some species reduce diversity, especially when subsidised at unnaturally high levels by human detritus – as crows and magpies are. And foxes are subsidised by introduced prey (rabbits) as well as free of natural enemies (wolves).

28. The Moral Terrorism of Animal Rights*

"Before graduating to mass-murder and necrophilia, Jeffrey Dahmer mutilated birds, rodents and domestic animals (the bones were found in a hut next to his father's house). The torture of small mammals is a regular occurrence in Britain. Rabbits are hung from trees. Squirrels are nailed to them. Hedgehogs are used as footballs. None of this, however, is illegal. The Wild Mammals (Protection) Bill will make it so."

Without wishing to defend cruelty to animals (or Dahmer), isn't this advertisement, placed in newspapers this month by the International Fund for Animal Welfare, just a little over the top? For a start, the Bill, to be voted on this week, says nothing about birds or domestic animals, and specifically exempts rodents from some of its clauses; so almost all Dahmer's juvenile activities would still be legal were somebody to copy them here after the Bill became law.

By heading the ad "What sort of person mutilates small animals?", the IFAW is trying to imply that anybody who does the things that would be banned by the Bill – ie, any fox-hunter – is a potential mass-murderer of people. That is not just fanciful; it is demonstrably untrue. As far as I know, no fox-hunting man or woman has ever become a mass-murderer. Even if one has, where is the evidence that it was the hunting that drove him or her to it? You could just as plausibly argue that if Jeffrey Dahmer had spent a few bracing days a week galloping across Leicestershire, he might not have had the inclination to murder.

The point I am disputing is not whether cruelty to animals is wrong; the point is whether in support of a campaign, however noble, you should stoop to such depths as to accuse your opponents of being potential mass murderers. After all, I could take out an advertisement as follows: "What sort of people support the International Fund for Animal Welfare? Before

---

* Published as 'Shock of the untrue' in *The Sunday Telegraph* on 25 February 1995.

graduating to genocide, Adolf Hitler was especially concerned about cruelty to small animals…"

Of course, by discussing the advertisements I am granting them still more publicity. Advertising executives are, even as you read this, faxing each other congratulations on the success of provoking me into giving their campaign free time on the page. That, after all, was the purpose of Benetton's shocking posters of a few years ago; they had nothing to do with clothes but everything to do with provoking debate about them in which the brand name got lots of mention – as it is getting now.

There simply is no limit to how shocking an advertisement should be if it is to be effective, so long as it is not defamatory (note: Jeffrey Dahmer is dead). There have been several complaints to the Advertising Standards Authority, but as far as the client is concerned, the more complaints the better. The Wild Mammals (Protection) Bill will almost certainly not become law, yet the IFAW has spent £500,000 on newspaper advertising alone, and as much again on other forms of campaigning. It may prove money well spent for the organisation, which will hope to recoup a good return on the investment in terms of donations, subscriptions and new people to send direct mail to.

The discovery that pictures of mutilated animals in newspaper advertisements can raise large sums was made during the late 1980s when oiled birds in Alaska and tuskless elephant corpses in Africa produced huge dividends for environmental groups. The full-page elephant ads of 1988 advocating an ivory ban were among the few that have ever produced more immediate donations on torn-out coupons than they actually cost.

Biafra had first revealed that pot-bellied starving children had the same effect for Third World poverty charities, and quite rightly they milked them for all they were worth. But the public palate gets jaded, and to be effective the image has to be more and more shocking or imaginative. The staring eyes of a starving child do not work so well any more. The same has happened in the animal-welfare field. There is competition between the organisations to be more shocking and imaginative.

So, not to be outdone by IFAW, the Royal Society for the Prevention of Cruelty to Animals produced an astonishing advertisement suggesting to people: "As the law stands you could put down this magazine, go outside and play football with

76

a live hedgehog." It had not occurred to me until then. Luckily the idea does not appeal to me. I could go out and do all sorts of things. I could go out and squirt soapy water at a blackbird (and still could after the new Bill had become law).

Apparently the RSPCA did bring a case to court in 1991 concerning two youths in Faversham, Kent, who shot a hedgehog with an air rifle six times, used it as a football and threw it on a bonfire. They got a ticking-off from the magistrate for their "horrific cruelty". I hope they got an even worse ticking-off from their parents. Under the new Bill, which specifically outlaws "kicking" a wild animal, they could in theory have been fined or imprisoned for up to six months; in practice, being juveniles, they would have got a ticking-off from the magistrate.

Is it not better that the youths should have been breaking some law than not? After all, badgers are already protected from cruelty by law; why not hedgehogs? This is the crux of the issue. Badgers are threatened by a popular, if disgusting, pastime called badger-baiting that would flourish if it were not illegal. Hedgehogs are very rarely threatened by the occasional pervert who is sick enough to enjoy kicking them; a law would be most unlikely to deter him (the RSPCA says there have been a few other cases of hedgehog-kicking, but cannot produce chapter and verse). That is a vital difference.

The reason for the Bill is that its supporters believe that foxes are so cruelly treated in the course of hunting for sport and snaring for pest control that those activities should be treated, like badger-baiting, as torture and outlawed. Fair enough: let us have a debate about that. It is a reasonable position to adopt. But of the seven full-page advertisements I have seen from the RSPCA and the IFAW, not a single one even *mentions* fox-hunting. It is, in ad-shock terms, old-hat. They all go on and on about kicked hedgehogs, nailed squirrels, accidentally snared domestic cats and Jeffrey Dahmer, which are at best side-issues, at worst red herrings. Why are they so afraid of the main issue? If we are going to outlaw activities, let us at least be honest about which ones and why. We did not make murder illegal because it might be accompanied by torture, but because it is wrong in itself.

When I made some of these points to the RSPCA, I was angrily accused of supporting animal torture, which illustrates just how hard it can be to have a debate with somebody who can claim moral indignation on his side. So here is my morally indignant riposte. It is disgusting and disgraceful that the RSPCA and IFAW have not lifted a finger to campaign on behalf of wild birds, which are lured to bird tables with peanuts, then caught by domestic cats and taken half alive to be tortured; the animals' owners are in full knowledge of what the cats are doing with their blessing. There should be a law against keeping cats.

29. The Unprecedented Power of Pressure Groups*

At one point last week Oxfam and two other charities threatened to withdraw from the poverty summit in Copenhagen because they were not being sufficiently consulted during the preparation of the final document. Since the whole point of these United Nations global jamborees – Rio, Cairo, now Copenhagen – is to provide a platform for pressure groups to embarrass politicians, they may have a case. But it is worth pausing to recognise just how much pressure groups, who prefer to be called 'NGOs', are included in policy making already.

The world summits are trade fairs for pressure groups. I know this because I have never been to one of them. Therefore, unlike the wretched politicians who trundle off thinking the real business of the summit is what goes on in the high-level meetings, I know how the summits actually come across to the public. What the world got from Rio, Cairo and Copenhagen was a series of pressure groups being interviewed by reporters to comment upon the issues of the conference; the actual declarations might as well be in Linear B.

At these summits, moreover, any pressure group leader with his head screwed on in roughly the right direction knows exactly what script to read from. If he says something like 'We are glad this meeting is taking place and we applaud the measures already taken, but we recognise that there will be obstacles to putting more into practice', he can kiss good-bye to his slot on the *Today* programme. It works better to say: 'The third world is being betrayed today by what is going on behind that closed door.'

I make no judgement about which pressure groups are right and which are wrong. I merely observe that the whole thing is good for all pressure groups and bad for all politicians. So why

---

* Published as 'Never mind the politics – feel the pressure' in *The Sunday Telegraph* on 12 March 1995.

are the politicians and diplomats so accommodating? Mostly, I suspect, because they are scared stiff of being criticised by these people. A bad report from Oxfam, Greenpeace, Compassion in World Farming, or Amnesty International can give a politician all kinds of trouble.

Bad reports can be earned not just for policies, but simply for excluding these groups from access to your office. The result is that – *contra* Oxfam's complaint – pressure groups are frequently, fully and excessively consulted by government. They are in and out of minister's offices the whole time, pausing only long enough between visits to pop up on the radio and criticise the minister to keep him scared.

Never has a government been so open to lobbying as the present British one. The handiwork of pressure groups can be seen in virtually every Bill it brings forward. They practically wrote the disastrous 1988 Criminal Justice Act, which had to be unravelled when its flaws became clear.

Even the bureaucracy defers to pressure groups. A planning application on a certain kind of listed building is nowadays automatically sent by local authorities to the Georgian Society (who elected it?). Pressure groups represent strands of public opinion, of course, so they argue it is meet and right that they should be consulted. Yet they represent extremists, not the silent majority, and they work by a highly undemocratic competition to shout loudest.

This is demagoguery. He with the most money makes the most noise, wins the most publicity and has most effect. Big business and quangos are rightly criticised for this. Let us just occasionally hear the media put the heat on the greatly more influential pressure groups. It would be good for them.

30. Central Planning in the Scottish Highlands*

Are we aware of – indeed, did we vote for – the nationalisation of heather? This government, castigated by Scottish voters for its adherence to principles of individualism, has suddenly and rapidly accelerated the trend towards the nationalisation of the Highlands of Scotland.

My evidence for this startling claim is illustrated by three news stories of the past few weeks. One was the purchase and endowment by lottery players of Mar Lodge estate, a substantial chunk of the Cairngorms and Deeside. This now passes from an American billionaire to the National Trust for Scotland.

The result is that instead of £10 million of private money coming into the Scottish hills to employ people, cover annual deficits, invest in improvements to the environment and so on, the same amount has had to be produced by the poor old lottery player. Greens often complain about their hills being playthings of the rich, but what a wonderful boon to the environment that fact has been. It has meant that private money has poured into Scotland to pay for keeping the hills wild for deer, grouse and walkers, and for keeping commercial forestry at bay, at no cost (and some benefit) to the Scottish taxpayer.

The second story was the brief flurry of excitement over the fact that none of the Balmoral estate next door to Mar Lodge is designated as a site of special scientific interest, because the Crown is exempt from such designation. Amid the sounds of great indignation from Friends of the Earth, it passed unnoticed that Balmoral is not noticeably the worse for ten years without such bureaucratic 'protection'.

Nor did anybody point out how horrendously counter-productive the whole policy of designation is. A landowner is punished for resisting the blandishments of thirty years of

---

* Published as 'Big Brother tightens grip on Highlands' in *The Sunday Telegraph* on 14 May 1995.

governments to rip out his hedges, drain his meadows and improve his moors by having the land designated, which means in effect nationalised. He must obey a management agreement drawn up by the state and see his land fall in value as a result, while his greedier neighbour is rewarded with no designation. Designation is a classic case of punishing the innocent and rewarding the guilty. It creates all the wrong incentives, but it also creates lots of work for bureaucrats and their parasitic greens, which is its purpose.

The third story, buried in Thursday's *Daily Telegraph*, contained the startling news that the Red Deer Commission was to be equipped with helicopters, a bigger budget and new powers to pursue and kill its charges, which will now include all species of deer. This is a classic example of how the bureaucracy grows. Originally established as an advisory agency, the commission has gradually succeeded in helping the government turn it into a sort of equivalent to a state wildlife department in America, with intrusive powers over private landowners to control what happens to the deer on their land.

The excuse is the deplorable state of the old Caledonian forest, which persists because of too many deer. But who originally got the forest in the bad state it is in? Not, as greens would have you believe, the deer, which are merely preventing regeneration now, but the government, which in the shape of the Forestry Commission ordered the felling of large areas of the forest during the last war, 'improved' (ie, tore out to replace with straight lines of sitka spruce) twice as much of the Caledonian forest in its ownership as private landowners did of the forest they owned, and, into the bargain, handed out tax breaks to private owners to destroy their forests too.

To the extent that the Highlands are environmentally attractive, the credit should go largely to private owners. To the extent that they have been spoiled, the blame lies almost entirely at the door of successive governments. So why nationalise them further?

31. The Shrill Cry of the Lesser Spotted Acronym*

A spring morning, high in the Pennines. Curlews, peewits and golden plover sing mournfully into the breeze, their plaintive cries catching the harmony of the wind. If only we could understand what they are saying.

But wait! We can. A brilliant new device from the University of Wensleydale Department of Ornitho-Acoustics has decoded a brief conversation between two birds held last month. Unfortunately, the machine then fell off the back of a Land Rover and has not worked since. The conversation went like this:

First curlew: Have you heard? MAFF has just designated this area as an ESA.

First plover: I thought it was an AONB.

FC: It is; and it's an AOHLV, too, but that does not mean it cannot also be an ESA. The farmers will now get extra money for looking after our habitat.

FP: Peewit says Snipe always takes care to nest in an SSSI, and swears by them. Can we do that?

FC: You can if you like, but only if you want scientists breathing down your neck all day. ESAs are better because the farmers get paid to leave us alone. Farmers hate sites of special scientific interest, because it just means their land's been confiscated by EN – that's English Nature – which then decides exactly how it should be managed. Most SSSIs are crawling with crows and foxes, anyway. And besides, it just shows how behind the times Snipe is. The fashionable people now refer to SSSIs as SCAs – special conservation areas; that's what they have become ever since the EU's Habitat Directive came into force.

FP: Talking of the EU, I saw a sign the other day covered in gold stars saying something about this area now being covered by Objective 5b. Any idea what that means?

---

* Published as 'Hark! The shrill cry of the lesser spotted acronym' in *The Sunday Telegraph* on 11 June 1995.

FC: Quite simple. The EU has lots of ECUs because of all the VAT it takes, and not all of it goes on the CAP, so it gives it to any farmer who wants to turn his barn into a hostel for hikers; that's Objective 5b. Everything not covered by Objective 5b is in Objective 2. The whole idea is to cover the countryside with gold stars so that gullible people are grateful for getting some of their own money back again from Brussels – minus a hefty chunk for expenses.

FP: Who decides how we get all these designations? It must be hard work.

FC: It is; that's why they like it – justifies their jobs and budget increases. Well, for ESAs it's MAFF but they take advice from ADAS, the NFU and CLA; for SSSIs it's DoE after taking advice from the JNCC, EN, ITE and NERC. But English Nature usually consults the RSPB first.

FP: There was some rumour about a factory going up in the valley, wasn't there? What happened to that?

FC: After the HSE and the EHOs closed down all the local businesses for failing to meet their new regulations, there was bad unemployment, so the locals were keen on the plan for a new factory. But the CPRE kicked up a huge fuss on behalf of the NIMBY incomers. So the RDC threw it out, on the grounds that it didn't fit with DOE's PPG13, let alone their local plan which had not designated this area as suitable for C2 uses. But the developer won on appeal to the SOS, who was probably lobbied by the DTI, which wanted the jobs. Then the developer couldn't reach agreement with the RDC on a Section 106 agreement, and the DOT refused to upgrade the road, so the whole scheme died of old age. Apparently, they built it in Taiwan instead.

FP: Well, at least they then leave us alone.

FC: That's the whole point. Nobody with any responsibility for the countryside has the time to come and look at us. They're far too busy pushing paper at each other and driving their desks. No acronym can afford to relax for an instant, lest another one get more money to spend.

32. How Red Tape is Strangling Red Squirrels*

Next week is, in case you had not heard, red squirrel week. It will culminate in a squirrel nutkin raft race on Derwentwater in the Lake District to commemorate the historic expedition of the red squirrels to Old Mr Brown's island, recorded in Beatrix Potter's book. Twelve rafts will take part in the race, with yours truly among the crew of one of them.

We northerners are very worked up about the inexorable retreat of the native red squirrel in the face of competition from the introduced grey. Along a line from Durham to Cumbria the greys are pushing steadily north to join up with their beachhead in the Borders. Lucky people like me who feed wild red squirrels in their garden every morning are living on borrowed time.

We are also increasingly worked up by the indifference shown on the issue by bureaucrats and conservationists. The conservationists, with some honourable exceptions such as the Northumberland Wildlife Trust, dare not touch the subject for two reasons. The first is that it looks like a losing battle: nobody has yet halted the march of the grey squirrel, and nobody likes the public relations risk of failure. That's presumably why Greenpeace is not burning grey squirrels in effigy in Trafalgar Square.

The second reason is that the culprit is not the evil chemical industry, but a furry animal itself. The only cost-effective way to save red squirrels is to selectively poison greys in specially designed traps that only greys can enter. This is anathema to groups who care more about animal welfare than conservation. Rather greys should cause the deaths of thousands of reds than that a single grey squirrel should suffer at the hands of man.

The bureaucrats have a different set of reasons for their indifference. The primary one is that almost all the decision makers are southerners based in the south. If grey squirrels were

---

* Published in *The Sunday Telegraph* on 6 August 1995.

spreading south from the north and had just reached, say, Peterborough, you can be sure public money would be pouring into the battle.

But also, by definition, bureaucrats follow rules, and in this case the rules say you may only poison grey squirrels in counties where reds no longer exist. It is a classic case of a rule that could not be better designed to encourage the decline of the red squirrel. Attempts to change this rule to allow the use of the selective poisoning traps to save red squirrels in the north have run foul of government lawyers, who would rather red squirrels died by the thousand from competition-induced starvation than run the risk that one died by mistake from poison.

Further evidence for this perversity of regulations came in two letters to *The Times* last week on great-crested newts. Lord Parmoor, the author of one of the letters, made the sensible point that the whole thrust of official policy, which is to delay at great cost any development that might threaten a newt-containing pond and punish anybody who handles a wild newt without a licence, is misguided. To promote newts we should instead be encouraging people to buy and sell great-crested newts for their new suburban garden ponds, rather than fighting a forlorn battle to save traditional farm ponds, which are disappearing anyway. You can now, in law, buy great-crested newts from dealers so long as they are captive-bred, but most dealers are unaware of this and still offer a foreign subspecies.

If the enemy of newts were say, a furry animal, and if the enemy of red squirrels were modern industry; if great-crested newts lived in the north and red squirrels in the south: would priorities be a little different? I wonder.

33. Greenpeace: A Cause
Driven by Cash Flow*

The South Sea Company was formed to raise money on the
London stockmarket in 1711; that – and not exploring the South
Seas – was its true mission. But it was so good at deceiving
investors into thinking that it was trading in the South Seas that
it gobbled up huge sums before the bubble burst.

Greenpeace, now playing to large audiences in the same seas,
is not dissimilar. It is an organisation devoted to growing as an
organisation; it spends most of its money not on the
environment, but on stunts, billboards, ships and salaries: self-
promotion.

After admitting last week that it thought a fish bumping into
its hydrophones, or a flatulent whale passing nearby, was a
nuclear explosion on Mururoa, Greenpeace can hardly be called
a scientific organisation. It also admitted, of course, that the
Brent Spar did not contain oil at all, let alone the 5,000 tons it
had insisted was there during its battle with Shell. This is
hilarious from an organisation which states in its latest
newsletter that 'The evidence contained in the Shell reports is
factually sparse and conjectural in nature.'

Nor is Greenpeace a political organisation. It loves
blackmailing politicians, true, but it is no think-tank, and rapidly
moves on from any issue where there is a threat that consensus
or reason might break out, and rarely makes detailed policy
suggestions.

Nor is Greenpeace an environmental organisation. It runs no
nature reserves, houses no endangered species, restores no
damaged ecosystems. It spends its money campaigning for other
people to do these things, not doing them itself. Compare it with
your local naturalist's trust.

So, if Greenpeace is not a scientific or a political or an
environmental organisation, what is it? The answer clearly is

---

* Published in *The Sunday Telegraph* on 10 September 1995.

87

that it is a commercial concern. It raises money from its members and donors with the intention of spending £90 million a year on things that will attract more members and donors while paying the salaries of its employees. It is the commercial equivalent of the South Sea Company: a company that spends all its money on raising more money.

According to *The Independent*, the Brent Spar campaign was born in a suggestion from a Greenpeace employee to mount a high-profile stunt to reverse the decline in membership of the previous few years. No doubt Greenpeace genuinely thought their stance was the right one, too, but the commercial imperative was plainly paramount (else why did Greenpeace not choose a less glamorous, but more important issue like overfishing in the North Sea). It worked like a dream until last week.

Likewise in the Pacific, Greenpeace knows that one more underground nuclear test to add to the 1,400 that have already been safely carried out pales beside the damage being done to (say) wandering albatrosses by Japanese-owned squid-fishing boats. But it also knows that donations will flow to the organisation that mounts the most high-profile campaign, gets on the news most often and provokes French commandos into most violence.

On the question of the Mururoa tests, I actually agree with Greenpeace. I no more want to support the French just to spite Greenpeace than vice versa. I think the nuclear tests are probably motivated by somebody in the French defence ministry protecting his departmental budget. I also think it represents the insulting worst of colonialism to do it in the Pacific rather than Corsica. Worst of all, the French government has now granted Greenpeace priceless publicity, radicalised the whole of Australia and made opposition to nuclear tests synonymous with supporting Greenpeace. It has behaved like a stockbroker promoting shares in the South Sea Bubble.

34. The Need for Conservation Entrepreneurs*

I have argued several times in these columns that government grants for conservation should go, not on buying chunks of good habitat to preserve it, but on buying chunks of bad habitat to restore it. My advice usually falls on deaf ears, but not always. The Royal Society for the Protection of Birds has just bought 600 acres of prime carrot fields to turn them into a reedbed. How splendid!

The carrot fields are in East Anglia and so long as it can find £1 million to pay for the land and the restoration (petty cash for the RSPB, with its £30 million annual budget), the fields will soon become a reserve called Lakenheath Fen. In a few years it will be reedbeds and grazed marsh, brimming with bitterns, bearded tits, marsh harriers and water rails.

The mentality of nature conservation is far too defensive, obsessed with protection rather than improvement. Conservation grants are needed in places that have been ruined: the canalised rivers, the flat, denuded farmland of the Fens, the spruce-infested square blocks of subsidised new forests, the terrible vandalism represented by hydroelectric dams in Scotland and Wales. Undoing these wrongs should be our aim, not slapping ever more bossy regulations on the few bits of our countryside that have retained their biodiversity and natural feel – usually thanks to sympathetic private owners prepared to ignore past official advice to ruin them. (For the second time in recent history, the government has just stimulated a rash of hedge removal, by the simple means of threatening to make it illegal.)

Perhaps the RSPB or some other organisation would like to take up the challenge, and sell into commercial hands those of its reserves that are profitable (with restrictive covenants), using the money to buy ugly, ruined landscapes and turn them into

---

* Published as 'A case of the good, the bad and the ugly' in *The Sunday Telegraph* on 17 September 1995.

fabulous new reserves. There are precedents. In Wisconsin, the Nature Conservancy sold a lakeside reserve, with covenants, to a firm that thought it could run the reserve profitably, and used the money to buy and protect a larger reserve for rare plants.

Attractive as this idea is, it could not happen on a big scale, for a simple one-word reason: government. Suppose you wanted to buy an ugly modern block of forestry and clear it away to make a heather moor or a wilderness woodland, you would be prevented by the government. You would have to apply for a felling licence, which would not be granted for an immature plantation. Once again, the bureaucratic imperative – regulate, regulate, regulate – stands in the way of real conservation, rather than encourages it.

Or suppose one of the privatised electricity generators, flush with cash, said it wanted as an environmental gesture to close down a hydro-electric scheme, remove the dams, allow rivers to flow naturally in their beds again and replace the generating capacity with some clean, efficient gas power stations with small, urban space requirements. Such an offer would be an unambiguous environmental good, but you can bet your bottom pound 'environmentalists' would campaign against it on the grounds that hydro power is 'sustainable' and produces no carbon dioxide. No matter that it also ruins some of the best scenery in the country in Wales and Scotland.

At present, entrepreneurial flair is handsomely rewarded by government subsidies for ruining landscapes with industry, forestry or agriculture. The only answer that bureaucrats and greens seem to have is to nationalise the right to do anything in the countryside and ban it. Far better, surely, to harness entrepreneurial flair for environmental ends. Give grants and promise the removal of regulatory restrictions on those who improve the landscape for wildlife, instead of doing the exact opposite.

35. How Ramblers Make Access to the Country Harder*

Today is the day of mass trespass by the Ramblers Association on behalf of their campaign to open all uncultivated land to unrestricted access. Ramblers think it is wrong that the person who owns a piece of land with no footpath across it has the right to say who may walk on it. They want to go everywhere not by permission, but by right.

If ever there was a countryside issue where strident polarisation has been the enemy of progress, access is it. Imagine if the Ramblers were an organisation devoted to negotiating access to private land on behalf of its members, at a price. Suppose they approached landowners and said: 'We know you own this moor, and that owning it costs you several thousand pounds a year in wages, taxes and other costs. So we are offering you a thousand pounds a year in exchange for the right for any member of our association to walk upon it. In return we will strictly enforce a policy of no litter, no dogs except on leads, no deviation from certain paths and no gates left open. We will then go back to our members and advertise it.'

The effect of such an offer would be dramatic. Landowners would fall over themselves to sign such agreements and would quickly come to respect the ramblers; ramblers associations would grow rapidly as the benefits of membership became apparent, and would quickly come to respect the rights and concerns of the landowner.

Instead we have a ridiculously politicised system in which there is no way for landowners to profit from public access. Indeed, quite the reverse: they pay heavy costs if they let people have unrestricted access. The costs take the form of piles of litter, gates left open, sheep worried, badgers dug up for badger

---

* Published as 'Can landowners forgive their trespassers' in *The Sunday Telegraph* on 24 September 1995.

baiting and birds' nests deserted, not to mention vandalism and noise from motorbikes.

Now this is most unfair to the average rambler, who is 55 years old and armed with nothing more offensive than slightly too-short shorts. But then Kate Ashbrook, head of the Ramblers, is even more unfair about the average landowner: 'I am today putting the path-blocking, anti-access, criminal, land-owning community on notice,' she said when campaigning for the job. The Ramblers never recognise or even say that the great majority of landowners not only do not block paths, they clear them, cut them, signpost them and respect them – often at some cost to themselves. The Ramblers Association pays not a penny towards this cost.

I once asked a party of 50-ish, beshorted, female ramblers walking a path on our farm to put their unruly dogs on leads. They refused on the grounds that there were no lambs about. This was not actually true – there were lambs in the very field they were crossing – but it indicated their curmudgeonly, confrontational and uncompromising attitude. To tar all ramblers with such a brush is no worse than to tar all landowners with the brush of blocking footpaths.

Like a general insisting on unconditional surrender, Kate Ashbrook has deliberately set herself such an impossible goal that she can be fairly confident it will never be achieved and therefore that her own job of demanding it is secure. Totally unrestricted access would be a disastrous thing for the countryside and everybody with an ounce of sense knows it.

The landowner, who has already lost the right to fell trees, build houses, and go fishing – without government permission – has only two real rights left un-nationalised. The first is to sell his property to whomever he chooses; the second is to allow permissive access off public rights of way to whomever he chooses. To remove that last right would render all uncultivated land no-man's land. No man would have an incentive to defend it against litter and despoliation. The state would have to take on the job. If you think that would work, count the polythene bags on motorway verges.

36. A New Empire is Built on Hadrian's Wall*

This month ends the consultation period for a new and ambitious plan: the creation of the Hadrian's Wall Military Zone. To those with very long memories this will induce a sense of *déjà-vu*.

Nearly two thousand years ago the land across which Hadrian's wall snakes was, presumably, peaceably owned by some bunch of local Pictish farmers. Imagine their astonishment when they woke up one morning to see a platoon of skirted infantry supervising slaves heaving stones on top of each other to build a gigantic wall straight across their best sheep fields.

'Oi!', they surely called, 'You there with the plumed helmet! What do you think you're doing? That pile of masonry's blocking my road to market.' For answer, there came only a clout about the ears with the flat of a sword. Relentlessly, ordered by an unelected fascist in Rome, the masonry spread across the landscape, disrupting lives, blocking trade routes, stealing land. Hadrian's Wall is a testament to the power of the state to ride roughshod over people's lives.

Today, exactly the same thing is happening. Northumbrian sheep farmers are waking up to find that their land is suddenly not to be theirs at all, but is part of the 'Military Zone', a band across Northern England that will henceforward be run by a committee. There are two small differences between English Heritage's present land grab and Hadrian's. The first is that English Heritage issued a consultation document first. It is uncertain if Hadrian did the same.

The second difference is that Hadrian was less greedy. He took only the land he needed for the actual wall itself and the road that ran alongside it. English Heritage wants a great swathe of land in places more than five miles wide and extending forty miles beyond the end of the wall, down the Cumbrian coast to include, bizarrely, the foreshore of Sellafield power station.

---

* Published in *The Sunday Telegraph* on 8 October 1995.

There is a third difference: that English Heritage is a democratic body entirely accountable to us, its political masters, and not concerned with empire building, only with disinterestedly conserving the landscape for future generations to enjoy. (Warning: this paragraph contains irony.)

What is the point of the Military Zone? It mostly covers areas that are greatly restricted by planning laws anyway: areas of great landscape value, outstanding natural beauty, scientific importance, national park, etc. There is about as much danger of somebody building a plastics factory on the wall as there was in 122 AD.

What would be different after the Military Zone came into force would be, first, that farmers would be subject to planning laws – the crops they planted and the animals they grazed could be vetoed by men in suits for spoiling the view – and, second, that a new and centralised bureaucracy would run the whole wall centrally. In other words, like everything Whitehall ever does, the aim is to centralise decision taking and remove it from local people.

It is all there in the document. The management committee it proposes would consist of representatives from ten quangos and ministries, four lobbying organisations and a couple of academic institutions. The 'co-ordination unit' that would actually take the decisions, is given eleven long paragraphs of detail about directors, offices and responsibilities.

By far the most exciting place near Hadrian's Wall is Vindolanda, the settlement from which the wall's original construction was overseen. It has yielded by far the largest haul of leather goods and handwritten documents from anywhere in the empire. The haul includes the earliest writing from anywhere in Britain and the earliest female handwriting in the world; it allows a glimpse into the soap opera of real life, not just major events. Vindolanda has been owned, protected, excavated and displayed entirely by private owners.

37. Oxford Cashes in on Doom-mongering*

'Even in thirty years' time, the world may hardly be recognisable because of the dramatic changes which are taking place. It is a frightening scenario, and for those of us with children it is even more disturbing – we think about their future as well as our own. We try to protect them, and help them succeed, but the changes in the world's environment seem out of our control.'

This remarkable paragraph came in a letter I received last week. The letter was trying to scare me into giving money. It was full of really frightening assertions. 'By 2050,' it said, 'a third of all agricultural land in England and Wales will probably become marginal.' Droughts, floods and windstorms may be twice as common in the next century as they are now. Last summer's drought represented 'the shape of things to come'. 'We have already begun to see the effects of such changes in increased skin cancer and asthma'. And so, terrifyingly, on and on.

We have come to expect such letters from the loonier green organisations. They play fast and loose with the known facts, make wild extrapolations, speculate in ways that are wholly unjustified by any form of science and bury little words like 'may', 'seem', 'up to' and 'probably' in their sentences lest somebody like me challenges them. The letters are written, we all know, by their fund-raisers, not their scientists, who hold their noses as they sign these mendacious pieces of propaganda. No reputable scientists claims that skin cancer is increasing because of environmental change.

Hardly a single one of the assertions made in the letter in question can be called a fact. All the extrapolations are based on only the most alarmist assumptions, not the consensus of opinion. I could just as reasonably and with just as much

---

* Published as 'Why profits of doom can't stop change' in *The Sunday Telegraph* on 29 October 1995.

evidence write a fund-raising letter saying the exact opposite of every statement in the letter, except for the bits about how we like our children. I dare say I would raise less money, but I would tell no more fibs.

As I say, loony greens after my wallet again. No surprise there. But which loony greens were these? The letter came from (or rather was signed by) the Pro-Vice-Chancellor of Oxford University. It was after money from Oxford graduates for the university's development programme. The excuse was that there is at Oxford something called the Environmental Change Unit, which is a bunch of mostly sensible scientists doing mostly sensible things to justify the fact that they have geography degrees. They have more integrity than the fund-raising letter implies, surely.

The word 'change' has changed its meaning recently. A decade or two ago people reluctantly accepted that the world changed all the time and never stayed the same. The climate changed, technology changed, tastes changed, and there was nothing we could do about it. Now marketing executives have discovered how much people dislike change and how potent it is to tell them they can stop it.

The climate has always changed. There is no such thing as a pristine climate. What do we count as Britain's 'normal' climate? The cold winters of 1700, the hot summers of 1200, the vicious cold of the last ice age, the tropical swelter of some of the interglacials when hippos swam in the Thames? What is Britain's natural vegetation? Tundra, birch woods, pine forests, oak woods or open fields? It has had all five in only the last 10,000 years for roughly equal amounts of time.

Yes, Oxford, the world will change. No, it is not something to be deplored or apologised for. No, giving you money will not stop it. Study it by all means, but don't exaggerate your powers just to get people's money.

38. The Nationalisation of the Countryside*

It is time to revive the cult of Robin Hood. Even if the fellow never existed, he is more relevant today than for many centuries, for he was originally a champion of the local against the power of the state. His modern equivalent is a smallholder drowning in paperwork; the modern equivalent of the sheriff of Nottingham is the besuited man from the government coming to tell him what he cannot do.

I have been reading two fascinating books: Oliver Rackham's *History of the Countryside* and Simon Schama's *Landscape and Memory*. They made suddenly clear to me what the word 'Forest' meant in medieval times. A Forest was not necessarily a place of trees, but a place of deer, a place where the king had asserted special forest law over a large chunk of the countryside in order to have a supply of venison to feed his court for free.

Says Rackham: 'As with a modern National Park, it would have been necessary to define the boundaries – in effect to put up notices saying "This is a Forest" – and to set up a bureaucracy of justiciars, seneschals, wardens, Foresters-of-fee, verderers, riding-Foresters, foot-Foresters, etc.' Everything went on as before in the new Forest, except that there was now a new set of potentially draconian laws about what you could and could not do. It was just like a modern National Park.

Quite quickly, the Plantagenet kings began to realise that they had a money-spinner on their hands. All sorts of ancient things that people did in the forest, like cut timber or feed swine, now required buying a pardon from the Forest courts. The forest bureaucrats saw themselves as a sort of Next Steps agency, required to raise as much money as possible. Shades of the National Rivers Authority, which has more than quadrupled the cost of a fishing licence in recent years even for people who own, look after and invest in their own fisheries.

---

* Published as 'Ride through the glen again, Robin Hood' in *The Sunday Telegraph* on 26 November 1995.

In 1308, one Robert Hood was forced to pay for wood he had cut in the forest of Wakefield. Being a loyal chap, he blamed not the king but the quango acting in the royal name, which was chaired by the fatcat sheriff of Nottingham, and put up something of a fight. The rest, as they don't say, is myth.

Earlier this month, the House of Lords debated the government's Rural White Paper, and Lord Selborne made a most perceptive speech. He welcomed the White Paper because of its emphasis on local solutions and local priorities. The countryside, he said, should be shaped 'bottom up' by the needs and decisions of local communities, not dictated from on high by central planners and distant bureaucrats.

Yet the bureaucracy will, I confidently predict, ignore the White Paper and continue its relentless 'top-down' approach to the countryside. Planners will churn out their indigestible and obsolescent structure plans, drafted to suit vested interests. Planning permission will be increasingly something that has to be purchased from these planners (the euphemism for such corruption is 'planning gain'). English Nature will continue its relentless 'designation' of those bits of the countryside not yet spoiled, thus effectively confiscating them from the owners who have taken care not to spoil them. MAFF has already half-nationalised farming; English Heritage is hellbent on nationalising the Roman Wall; the National Rivers Authority on nationalising rivers; the Countryside Commission on nationalising common land; the Forestry Commission on nationalising and afforesting moorland; and so on and on.

In every case the decision making is shifted from local people with boots on to central people with suits on. And the result will be just as unjust as the royal land-grabs of the twelfth century 'Forests'. Who will be the new Robin Hood, and object?

39. Vested Interests and Global Warming*

Appropriately for a cold week, tomorrow sees the start of a week-long meeting in Rome of the Intergovernmental Panel on Climate Change, the quango-cum-travel-agency for those whose salaries depend on keeping the world worried about global warming. Last week, in Madrid, they came to two remarkable conclusions.

The first one got plenty of media coverage, as it was intended to: global warming is definitely man-made. By this they mean that two computers, one British and the other German, programmed to blame global warming on man-made carbon dioxide and correct it for the cooling effect of man-made sulphur dioxide, now accurately mimic the inaccurately measured changes in global temperature over the past century or so.

Since the magnitude of the sulphur effect put into the computers was arbitrarily chosen to give the right result, this is no great surprise. (GINGO, as they say in computer speak, or garbage in, garbage out.) Climate change this century has so far been no greater than in most centuries, yet are we asked to assume that natural climate change mysteriously ceased this century and was replaced by man-made change?

The second conclusion from Madrid was ignored by the media. The IPCC has now downgraded its estimate of global warming by a massive 33 per cent. Three years ago it said the world would be three degrees warmer plus or minus 1·5 degrees in 2100. Now it says two degrees plus or minus one.

This is not the only figure to get steadily less alarmist as the facts come in. Satellites suggest no trend at all in temperature over 17 years. Carbon dioxide levels in the atmosphere unexpectedly *fell* in the early 1990s. And the 'official' effect of global warming on sea level has now been downgraded, yet again, to an increase of less than half a metre by 2100.

---

* Published as 'Climate debate is overheated and full of holes' in *The Sunday Telegraph* on 10 December 1995.

Temperatures rising a mere two degrees in a century, sea level rising by a little over a foot – the net effect on wealth and health would be small. Yet the IPCC working group on impacts is still working from the old figures. And even these new guesses may not be trustworthy: they are produced by people whose careers now depend on global warming.

When you tell environmentalists and scientists they have vested interests, too, they get cross. But they do. Imagine that you have been toiling away at atmospheric physics for thirty years in impoverished obscurity, and suddenly along comes global warming. Next thing you know the United Nations is paying you hundreds of pounds a day to sit in Madrid sampling the room service and appearing on *Newsnight*. Would you admit that the whole thing was nothing to worry about?

Scientists who dislike the way climate science has become a slave to political motives have recently banded together in the European Science and Environment Forum to express their doubts. They refuse to be bullied into declaring a conclusion before doing the research. For their pains they have been ostracised, deprived of access to data and accused of dubious motives.

Jack Barrett, an Imperial College chemist, is one of them. He concludes that, even on IPCC's figures, a doubling of carbon dioxide would increase global temperature by 0·2 degrees not two degrees; and that man-made emissions add just 3 per cent to the natural flux of carbon between the ocean, the continents and the atmosphere; tiny variations in this natural flux could swamp mankind's activities.

I still think man-made global warming is probably real, but since I first wrote alarmist articles about it ten years ago, it has grown steadily clearer that the effect will be slight rather than severe. When facts change, I change my mind. I have yet to meet a professional environmentalist with the same attitude.

40. Of Suits and Sandals*

Even plashy-footed nature columnists eventually get stale and start repeating themselves. To prevent this, I decided some months ago to cease writing this column before the end of this year, and so this is my last 'Down to Earth' column. From next week, the space will be filled by the capable pen of Deborah Devonshire.

Perhaps, too, I am running out of people to upset. Most greens already think I am an unprincipled apologist for polluters, most officials think I am prejudiced to the point of unhingement against government bureaucrats and at least one duke thinks I am quite unfair to sitka spruce trees.

This column began as a nature column but it soon became also a weekly comment on a large, complacent and growing industry: the nature industry. This consists of a symbiotic mixture of bureaucrats and lobbyists – suits and sandals.

The clever thing about this industry is that the public does not realise it exists. The public – simpleton that it is – thinks that conservationists conserve nature. This is like saying footballers score goals: it is the aim, but it is a poor description of what most of them spend most of the match doing. Most conservationists can and do talk for hours to each other without mentioning an animal or plant. I have seen them do it many times. They talk about committees, guidelines, grant applications, advertising campaigns, legislation, conventions, protocols, conferences, secretariats, treaties, regulations, resources – just like the businessmen they affect to despise.

This is true whether they are suits or sandals. The name of the game is much the same for all of them – diverting some of the money that flows into the environmental industry their way. Suits do it by giving themselves taxpayers' grants to administer and regulations to enforce. Sandals do it by winning grants or by persuading the public to make donations.

---

* Published as 'A parting shot at those suits and sandals' in *The Sunday Telegraph* on 17 December 1995.

The rare few in conservation who remain naturalists and can tear themselves away from desks and photocopiers long enough to get their boots muddy and actually do something are soon doomed to impoverished obscurity, for little of the money reaches them. The suits and sandals are far too good at intercepting it along the way. The route to fame and wealth is behind the desk.

Shortly before he died, Gerald Durrell was heard to mutter at a conference of conservationists something to the effect of: 'Talk, talk, talk – that's all conservationists do these days. In my day we used to get drunk with the natives.'

The point this column has tried again and again to make is that it need not be like that. Nature can be conserved and enhanced without channelling money through the hands of so many greedy suits and sandals. All it takes is the careful devolution of responsibility and the rejigging of economic incentives, and then local people will conserve nature naturally – be they farmers, businessmen or natives.

No green really wants the rain forest to belong to the Indians because then there would be no point in lobbying government about it. No official or lobbyist really wants the absurd Common Agricultural Policy abolished for the sake of nature; they just want the same money 'redirected into conservation' – ie, passed through their hands.

To them nature is not a joyful and fascinating subject of study but a 'task' – to be regulated, nationalised, planned and used as a ladder to the moral high ground. Most of these people seem to regard the production of a hefty 'plan' as an end in itself. Not for them the drafty bird hide at dawn; rather the cosy photocopier.

To paraphrase Oliver Cromwell, 'You have sat here too long for any good you have been doing. Devolve, I say, and let us have done with you.'

IEA Studies on the Environment

1. Roger Bate, Julian Morris, *Global Warming: Apocalypse or Hot Air?*, ISBN: 0-255-36331-1, 54pp., March 1994 (2nd Impression August 1994), £5·00.

2. Ike Sugg, Urs Kreuter, *Elephants and Ivory: Lessons from the Trade Ban*, ISBN: 0-255-36342-7, 74pp., November 1994, £7·00.

3. Matt Ridley, *Down to Earth: A Contrarian View of Environmental Problems*, ISBN: 0-255-36345-5, 80pp., February 1995, £8·00.

4. Michael 't Sas-Rolfes, *Rhinos: Conservation, Economics and Trade-Offs*, ISBN: 0-255-36347-8, 69pp., April 1995, £6·00.

5. Julian Morris, *The Political Economy of Land Degradation*, ISBN: 0-255-36348-6, 108pp., May 1995, £9·00.

6. Mark Pennington, *Conservation and the Countryside: By Quango or Market?*, ISBN: 0-255-36379-6, 68pp., April 1996, £6·00.

For further information on these and other IEA publications please contact: The Marketing Manager, Institute of Economic Affairs, 2 Lord North Street, London SW1P 3LB.

Down to Earth
A Contrarian View of Environmental Problems

MATT RIDLEY

---

1. World population growth is decelerating; food, oil and copper are all cheaper and more abundant than ever before.

2. Global temperatures may actually be falling, according to satellite sensors.

3. The ozone layer is getting thicker, not thinner, over temperate latitudes.

4. Winter sown corn, not pesticide use, is responsible for the decline in songbirds on farmland.

5. Some scientists say 20 per cent of species will be extinct in 30 years, yet the actual extinction rate of birds and mammals is 0·00008 per cent a year.

6. Big-game hunters are the best hope for the survival of Africa's wildlife outside a few well-financed national parks.

7. Environmental lobbying organisations are spending more money on lawyers and marketing men to grow their own budgets and less on naturalists and volunteers.

8. Forty per cent of all trees in Britain belong to the government, whose record of mismanagement of forest ecology, public access and finance is second to none.

9. Government conservation schemes are too defensive; their sole aim is to protect rich habitats rather than to improve impoverished ones.

10. Exaggeration, nationalisation and central planning are the enemies of the environment, not the allies.

IEA Studies on the Environment No. 3

Institute of Economic Affairs
2 Lord North Street
London SW1P 3LB

Telephone: (0171) 799 3745
Facsimile: (0171) 799 2137

£8.60 inc. p + p

ISBN 0-255 36345-1